She is Magic, Yes

A Magical Collaboration of 11 Women Sharing their Magic with the World

Magical Book Series
Blair Hayse Publishing
a Division of Blair Hayse,
International, LLC

First Edition

This book is dedicated to all those who have magic inside them and use it to profoundly impact the world around them. I truly believe that every person has magic in them, whether they have realized it or not. I encourage you to dig deep and find that magic. Use it to spread hope to the world around you and sprinkle it wherever you may go.

So, do not be fooled, I promise,

there is magic within each of you.

Enjoy the magic in the pages within...

Table of Contents

Foreword

Jennifer Kirch

Words are magic. Our words have so much power we don't even realize. With them, we have the ability to transform our life and the lives of others. In the pages that follow, you will have the opportunity to step into the lives of twelve magical men and women.

In the world today, there is so much divisiveness, uncertainty and negativity. In the midst of a global pandemic, Blair trusted her intuition and published the first volume of *She is Magic* sprinkling inspiration, positivity and hope in the world.

Yet, she didn't stop there. Continuing to inspire, two more editions in the *She is Magic* series were published during 2020. Now, this new volume some special men have opened up and shared their magic with the world.

All allowed themselves to be vulnerable and opened up their lives to share with you their experiences, some so raw that you wonder how they found the strength to go on. No matter what life continued to hand to them, each found their own way of taking painful circumstances and transforming it into inspiration.

"One day you will tell your story of how you overcame what you went through and it will be someone else's survival guide." ~ Brené Brown

These authors didn't simply stop to ask why this was happening to them, they looked to see what they could learn from it. Instead of staying in a victim role, they realized that having the right mindset and attitude could literally save your life.

Perhaps a particular story personally speaks to you as there are themes touching on addiction, domestic abuse, weight loss, struggles of societal norms, finding the positive in the pandemic, abandonment, divorce, bullying, helping a child overcome challenges, psychosomatic disorder, losing a loved one to cancer, and more.

"Magic is believing in yourself, if you can do that, you can make anything happen." ~ Johann Wolfgang Von Goethe

In summary, this book:

It is filled with optimism.
It is filled with healing.
It is filled with authenticity.
It is filled with vulnerability.
It is filled with love.
...and of course, it is filled with magic.

*-Jennifer
Kirch
February
2021*

Introduction

Blair Hayse

When I began the magical book series, I had a vision of helping women discover their magic within and be able to share it with the world around them. As we launched the first book of the series, in the middle of a global pandemic, I worried if I had made the right decision. I was met with a resounding, *YES!* The book climbed the charts to #1 on Amazon within hours of the launch. People craved the inspiration in a time we needed it most. People craved the magic found within the pages. I was thankful that so many people found that the book helped them to heal, inspired them and encouraged them to find their own magic. Just like that, an iconic series of magic was born.

This past year I was intrigued with the number of men that asked me to create a magical book that included them. After a lot of thought, *They are Magic* was born. A book that included everyone. Men. Women. Non-binary. An all-inclusive book of magic. The response to become authors was amazing as always and we set out to form the first book in our new magical series.

I am always amazed at the synchronicity of the authors that come together for each collaboration book. People from all walks of life. People from all over the world. All brought together by universal divine appointment of a being greater than all of us. As we join hands and go on the journey of publishing a book, I see the common strands of their stories come together. Most never knew the other before this journey, yet their stories intertwine so magically. It is all part of the magic I cannot explain.

As I poured over the stories in this book, I was brought to tears. As always, I am so amazed at the strength of these men and women. The sheer determination they found within them to rise to levels I cannot even comprehend. The stories they share. The authenticity and vulnerability they peel back to reveal to our readers. They choose to stand up and bring to you readers stories of inspiration in a world that is often filled with negative news. I am so grateful they trusted me to help them on this journey and to be witness to their magic. I love each and every one of them deeply.

For me personally, I love to write. It helps me to process my emotions and gives me an outlet to heal. It allows me to share my inner thoughts and to bring to life a story of magic that only words can do. Being able to create a series where I can do this with a group of empowering women, has been magical in itself. The publishing process and journey to bestselling author is like no other. It is filled with a roller coaster of emotions and ends with an adrenaline twist that is out of this world on launch day. It is addictive in a way. Hence why I am drawn to write over and over. Also, it is why I have repeat authors come into my books many times again. It is a supernatural experience that I cannot even put into words. I love being able to witness authors go through it for the first time and see how it transforms them. I honestly love my job.

I want to say thank you to you as a reader. As we launch this book, I assure you, that there will be many more to follow. The response to these books have been phenomenal. We are grateful for each reader who makes this journey possible for our team. We are blessed to know that you are enjoying the books and that you want them to continue. We hope to continue to bring stories of inspiration to you, so that you can be filled with magic time and time again. We welcome you to reach inside yourself as you read this book; to find your own magic within.

I want to say a thank you to all the men and women who filled this book, because I know how brave and vulnerable you had to be in order to share these stories. I am so proud of each of you for being willing to use your stories to help others. I want to say thank you to my graphic designer Lane who created a beautiful cover for the book that perfectly represents me, my brand and the message this book conveys. She never disappoints me and is always willing to help me graphically portray my messages in the best way possible. I want to say thank you to my assistant Samantha for all her hard work in helping me put this book together, working alongside all the authors and getting it ready to submit for publishing. Thank you to my virtual assistant Liz, who always gets me ready with graphics for the authors and launch day. Huge thank you to Amanda, my editor on staff for her amazing work and editing skills. Thank you to Janet for her hard work in helping the book be formatted correctly and loaded under all the right places.

I am forever grateful to my parents David and Teresa who encouraged me to always pursue my passion of writing. Thank you to my children Parker, Millie and Jackson who are the sunshine of my life and inspire me in more ways than they could ever know. Thank you to my husband Jeremy, who always believes in me when even the world thinks I am crazy! I would not be here without his support and encouragement. Thank you to my nanny Amanda, who without you watching over my home and child, I would not have the energy to pursue my aspirations in the speed in which I do so. Thank you to my current coach Crystal, who encourage me to pursue my talents and believe in me when I don't believe in myself. Thank you to my spiritual advisor Kristal who holds space for me and helps me to seek divine guidance in all I do. I love each and every one of you deeply. You hold the keys to my magic in so many ways.

If you are looking for something to read that is going to make you cry and laugh at the same time because it is so raw...then this book is for you. You will literally feel the emotions intertwined throughout these stories as you read them. These men and women held nothing back as they shared with you some of their innermost struggles, points of healing, lowest moments and highest accomplishments. They are authentic throughout their stories. They take you on the journey with them and you will not want to put it down as you begin to read.

As you read, be aware of your own stories found inside of you. Be aware of how sharing that story can inspire others and give others hope. It is more than just a "story." It is a journey of victory. It is a story of magic that you can sprinkle wherever you choose to go. Leave others with hope and inspiration just by being you.

Never…I repeat…NEVER…hide your magic.

You are Magic.

Magical Stories

It's All About Perception

Christine D'Elia

When I was a young trial attorney working for the New Jersey Division of Criminal Justice, I had the privilege of co-chairing my first trial, a terroristic threats case. The case involved a mentally unstable defendant who had made threats to a police detective and a judge through a phone call to a prosecutor's receptionist. The reason he had threatened their lives was because he felt his plea deal, which he had agreed to in court, was too harsh. The plea deal allowed this man to enroll in a Pretrial Intervention Program and avoid not only jail time but also a criminal record, despite the fact that he misused public property while working in the public sector. It was a great deal.

Nevertheless, the man called the prosecutor's office, threatened the officials involved in the case, and now he wanted to go to trial. I was happy to oblige and participate in my very first criminal trial as a deputy attorney general on behalf of the State. Since I was inexperienced and had only been writing legal briefs and arguing before the appellate courts up until that point, I was to be second chair. This meant that I was to assist the main attorney and I would not have as big a part in the trial as the main attorney. My supervisor, an older gentleman with graying hair, was the main attorney, or first chair, in this trial. He indicated that I would only be questioning a few witnesses during the trial, while he would be questioning the rest of the witnesses and presenting the opening and closing arguments. He also let me argue the legal motions mid-trial. Although I learned a lot during that first trial, the most important lesson came before it started, at a meeting with the judge and defense counsel.

You see, the judge and the defense attorney were also older men like my boss, and when I arrived 15 minutes prior to the start of the meeting, they were already in the judge's chambers discussing the case without me. At first, I was mortified. It was 8:45 in the morning. Had I gotten the time wrong? I could have sworn the law clerk scheduled the meeting for 9:00 a.m. As I walked into the room, the men kept talking, as though they did not even notice me standing there in my crisp navy suit and high heels, trial file in hand. At some point, the judge acknowledged my presence and indicated that he was already apprised of the facts of the case. The only thing left to discuss was the motions. I could not believe I missed a significant part of the pre-trial meeting on my first trial. I was embarrassed and annoyed.

After the meeting, as my boss and I were heading to the parking lot, I pulled him aside and asked what time the meeting had been scheduled to start. He stated, "Nine o'clock." That was when my embarrassment turned to anger. How dare he allow the meeting to start without me! I was an attorney of record on the case. I would have added value to the meeting, and I should have at least been able to hear what the defense counsel presented as his version of the facts. When I expressed my anger at the situation, my supervisor asked why I was so "upset." At that, I launched into an explanation about how it appeared that because I was a woman, and a young one at that, I was not considered a relevant part of the meeting, or even the case. I had familiarized myself with the facts and the law surrounding the case. I was prepared and on time. I should not have been excluded. In fact, I had arrived 15 minutes early. Was it really such an effort for them to wait for me? It was as if the young female attorney was of no consequence to the proceedings, or even welcome for that matter.

To my boss' credit, he did not dismiss me or try to defend their actions. What he said to me at that moment has stayed with me to this day. He explained that he had not thought about the fact that I was being excluded, or that I would perceive the start of the meeting without me as an exclusion. He said, "Perception is everything," and he even apologized for allowing the meeting to start without me.

The trial proceeded without any further slights, although I made sure I was at the courthouse by 8:00 a.m. from that day forward. Since I was only co-counsel, my main role in the trial was to research any legal issues that came up and then to argue our side to the judge. Although the defendant was only charged with terroristic threats, a third degree crime, I realized that the facts warranted a lesser-included charge of "retaliation for past official conduct." After all, the defendant had threatened the police detective and the judge in his original case because he was not happy with the way they officially handled it. I argued the motion for the additional charge and I won. That charge would be added to the case and given to the jury at the end of the trial.

At trial, the defense counsel argued that the defendant, that is, the man who called up a prosecutor's office threatening to kill a judge and a police detective, was merely a harmless "gadfly" and not a real threat. The counter-argument my boss made was that the defendant used the word "kill" and said he knew where the victims lived, which made this a credible threat. In the end, the jury found the defendant not guilty of the terroristic threats charge but convicted him of the lesser-included charge, the one I had successfully argued should be included in the case. I was more than happy with the outcome.

It has been over 20 years and over 30 trials since I tried my first case, but the lesson still resonates with me. Initially, I thought of how important it was to be aware of how my supervisors, co-workers, judges, and juries perceived me. To a large extent, it shaped how I presented my cases, comported myself at meetings, and supervised younger attorneys. However, the magic came from my ability to change my own perception of myself, especially in the face of adversity. When judges, defense attorneys, and even the press attacked everything from my clothing to my ethics during a hard-fought trial, I had to remind myself that I knew what I was doing was right. I pushed through the personal attacks and adverse rulings to fight harder for crime victims. It wasn't about me, so I had no time to wallow in self-pity or adopt a negative perception of myself. There was always a victim to rally behind and a valid argument to be found in support of our case. The magic I found was in my ability to shift my perception from negative to positive in times when I needed it most.

As time went on in my 25 year career as an attorney, I was always amazed when a victim, defense attorney, or judge offered up his or her unsolicited perception of me or my skills as an attorney. Some thought I was good attorney and had strong trial skills. Some criticized my techniques, saying I was too cautious and not assertive enough. Some thought I was too aggressive and hard. One female victim in a theft case told me I was "tough and cute as a button" in the hallway of the courthouse. Over the years, I've learned that it is good to take a temperature reading of how others perceive me, and it has sometimes helped me to adjust my attitude and actions accordingly. Even negative opinions were a helpful learning tool on most occasions.

After a long career and in the midst of a pandemic, I decided it was time to retire from my role as a prosecuting attorney. I was leaving a job that had 24/7 demands. I worked 12 to 13 hour days most weeks, on call at night and on weekends. Although I was looking forward to a rest, I was somewhat concerned with how to turn that off. There was also the fact that my father had been recently diagnosed with non-Hodgkin's lymphoma, and I wanted to spend more time with him. That made the decision easier, but the transition would not be. How would I perceive myself? What reality would I shape?

As my last workday drew nearer, I felt an overwhelming anxiety. Retirement is supposed to be a happy time, so why was I feeling this way? It led to a flurry of thoughts on how I would be perceived. Would I be criticized for retiring at a young age? Would people think I was giving up? If I did not take another job, would people think I was lazy or did not have what it took to practice law anymore? This job had been a large part of my identity for the past 25 years. I felt lost. I was already starting to miss my co-workers, whom I considered friends and not just colleagues. Would they remember me when I was gone? Who was I now?

I went into the office every day that last week. Yes, I even did work and attended Zoom meetings; old habits die hard. It was strange being one of the only people in the office, since most of my fellow attorneys were working remotely. There would be no retirement parties or even the traditional farewell happy hour this year due to COVID-19, although my amazing co-workers did organize a Zoom to say goodbye. It was in this forum that I got to see, yet again, how others perceived me.

When the meeting started, one of my esteemed colleagues Zoomed in from a zoo where she was spending the day with one of her children. She started off by saying that her family has a nightly ritual whereby her children, of which she has seven, go around the table and say something positive about each family member. She added that they cannot just say, "She's nice." It has to be something deeper, more specific. Following this explanation, my co-worker set the tone for my farewell Zoom and started off saying something positive about me, just like at her nightly dinners with her family. She told me that no matter how hard the job got or what trial difficulty I was dealing with, I always had a smile on my face when I greeted her, my adversaries, and my colleagues. She said that I was a warm person that made others feel warm. Her words brought tears to my eyes.

I had never thought of myself as "warm," especially at work. If you had asked me how I thought others perceived me, I would have said, "hardworking, honest, and direct, to the point of being blunt," and, I am sure more than a few perceive me as a "bitch." Although I have not polled the defense counsel, I am sure that would be a frontrunner.

After that attorney gave her "warm" assessment of me, a younger attorney spoke up. She was a 30-something blonde woman who had started at our office within the last two years. Although we did not work in the same unit, her office was close to mine. She said that I was always there for her when she was in trial and when hard questions came up. Specifically, she said she had been in the office at midnight during one of her first trials and came to my office because she knew I would be there to bounce ideas off of and work her trial issues out. She was grateful to me for being there to help with the problems that she had to address in court first thing the next morning. She perceived me as helpful and accessible.

By the end of that Zoom, I realized that the small things I had done throughout the years like smiling at my co-workers in the hallway and taking time out to answer fellow attorney's questions regardless of the hour of day were the most important. How we treat others is more important than the work we put forth or the number of successes we have.

Over time, and again throughout this touching farewell by my friends, I was reminded that how we perceive ourselves is where we find our magic. When I was down on myself or I thought others perceived me negatively, I was not confident. I recall that this was when I did my worst work and when I felt my worst. Throughout my career, I realized that it is not only important to perceive myself in a positive light but to be positive to others so that they can thrive and be confident.

As I write this chapter, over a month has passed since I retired from my job. I am no longer a prosecutor. At times, I feel like a ship that has come unmoored. It's time to drop the anchor and steady myself. The world is my oyster. I can create the life I want. That is my perception of retirement, creating a new chapter. My Magic comes from my ability to shape my perception, to create the reality of my dreams.

So, what is your perception of yourself? Is it positive, confident, and grateful for who you are? My experiences have taught me that when one perceives herself in a positive way, she cannot only increase her own self-confidence, but can change how others perceive her. I believe it is through this positive perception of ourselves that we all can create our own Magic.

About Christine D'Elia:

Christine was born and raised in New Jersey and grew up loving the beach. She earned her BS in Criminal Justice with a minor in Psychology at Trenton State College, which is now The College of New Jersey, in 1992. In 1995, Christine graduated cum laude from Seton Hall Law School. Following a judicial clerkship, she started as a deputy attorney general for the New Jersey Division of Criminal Justice.

In the first few years of her law career, Christine argued cases before the New Jersey Appellate Division and the New Jersey Supreme Court on behalf of the State. Thereafter, she worked in various trial sections, including the Gangs and Organized Crime Bureau, where she prosecuted traditional organized crime and gang racketeering cases. In 2007, Christine started at the Middlesex County Prosecutor's Office where she had the opportunity to work in a variety of units including the Special Victims Unit and Special Prosecutions Unit. While at the Prosecutor's Office, Christine tried rape and homicide cases, as well as white collar crime and official corruption cases. She also became a master trainer, training police throughout New Jersey in internal affairs policy and procedures.

At the end of 2020, after serving 25 years as a prosecutor and five years as section chief of the Special Prosecutions Bureau, she retired. Christine is excited to start a new chapter of her life with the publication of her first written work, *She is Magic, Yes*. She is hoping to continue writing and plans on traveling as much as possible.

To connect with Christine:

Email: seastheday3513@gmail.com

Facebook: https://www.facebook.com/christine.marie.3513

Butterfly Wings

Blair Hayse

Since childhood, a lot of messages come to me directly through dreams. Sometimes I know what the message is immediately while other times, I wake up to deeply analyze what was being conveyed to me. As a child, this gift scared me because I did not understand how I was able to dream things and then see them happen in real life. I had no one I could trust to talk to and carrying the burden was sometimes hard.

One incident comes to mind, where as a teenager I had a vivid dream of getting into a terrible argument with my dad over something I had not truly done. I remember waking up and knowing it was a warning that was going to happen soon. Within minutes, our house phone rang and I answered it because I could hear that my mom was in the shower. It was my grandmother, my dad's mom, and she had asked a question. After hanging up the phone, my mom and I got ready to go out to the home my parents were building at the time. When we got there, I remember my dad was so upset with me. He said my grandmother had told him that I was rude to her over the phone that morning. It spiraled into a terrible argument. I cried so hard afterwards, mainly because I knew it was going to happen and I couldn't stop it. As I grew older, my gifts remained. I learned how to lean into them and use them the best I could. Obviously, it still bothers me when I get dreams I cannot stop from happening.

About seven months ago, I was doing some branding photos in the beautiful downtown area of Atlanta. The photographer had taken a bunch of different shots and then asked if I had one of my books to use as a prop. I had packed our most recent *She is Magic, Too* book and pulled it out of my purse. She told me to flip it open so she could get a shot of me reading it over my shoulder. As I flipped open the book, it landed on the beginning of this beautiful co-author and dear friend of mine's chapter, Jennifer Kirch. "Written in the Stars" stared back at me from the title as the photographer snapped photos. In my gut, I knew it was a sign that we were connected in this book for a reason and that her magic was with me in that moment. It also immediately occurred to me that what was supposed to happen was indeed *written in the stars*. This particular author had struggled with cancer ever since I had known her, and she used her journey to help inspire others. After the photo shoot, I called her and asked her if I could please fly out to meet her in person. Even though there was no indication of it besides my serendipitous moment, I felt like time was limited.

Many months later, I had a dream about butterflies. It had come after the same co-author, Jennifer, had asked me what angle I felt she should take in her new chapter, for this particular book. She had written in every book and had been an editor on our team since the very first book was put together. I knew she needed to feel a fresh angle and new perspective. When the dream came, I immediately knew it was meant for her. The next day, I sent her a message that said, "I woke up the other night with the idea of doing it from the lenses of change, much like how you were talking to me the other day about how much has changed in just a year's time. Show them how it has changed. The good and the not so good, kind of like how a butterfly must go through changes. Let me know how that sounds." She immediately replied that funnily enough, she had a similar thought and would run with that idea.

For weeks I had trouble putting words into a chapter of my own. I sat down to write my chapter for this book several times and couldn't find any words that seemed to fit what I wanted to say. After numerous weeks of this pattern, I finally just shut down and decided it was not time for me to write it. I resolved to wait until the end of the editing process for the other chapters and try again, hoping the writer's block would pass by then. Little did I know that those next few weeks would not only bring me exact clarity on what I was supposed to write about, but that I would realize that the dream I had given Jennifer about butterflies was actually a direct message to me for my own writing. It was going to give me the material I needed to write on, but in a way, I did not want it to happen. Isn't life like that sometimes? Full of changes that propel us forward, but at the same time, ones we wish we did not have to face?

Fast forward exactly two weeks from the messages we had exchanged to a Sunday afternoon. I had slept most of the day away because I was exhausted and not feeling well. I woke up to a message from a mutual friend of mine and the co-author Jennifer shared, she was letting me know the Jennifer was placed in hospice and was unresponsive. I sobbed. I knew it was time to let go. I knew then why I had felt that moment seven months prior that time was limited, and I knew then why I had the dream about butterflies: she was about to gain her wings. I didn't want to face that reality because she was a pivotal influence in my writing career. She encouraged me, let me bounce ideas off of her, helped me edit, and reminded me of my magic when I had forgotten it. We sobbed on the phone together when things were not going well and we celebrated when they were. I couldn't really picture ever launching another book without her by my side and reminding me to just let the magic happen. I wanted to be selfish and hang on longer, but I knew in my heart that I had to let go. She was meant to gain her wings. All the signs had been given to me and I simply had not noticed them. I knew I had said all I wanted to say to her many times over. I had told her how I felt about her being in my life, that I was aware it was divinely orchestrated, and that I was grateful for the magic we were able to share. She also had left nothing unsaid. We had always reminded each other of the magic and love we shared.

The next morning, in the middle of my manager's meeting, I saw the text come across my screen that she had indeed received her wings. I cried. I took the day off and let myself grieve. I tried to process how I could keep her voice alive in the magic of my books as she would wish me to do. I tried to think of how I could honor her. I pleaded for her to give me a sign she was at peace, a sign that she was still with me. A week later, as I walked up the stairs to work, there on my doorstep was a beautiful, fluffy, white feather. Immediately, I knew that was my sign. As I sat down to write out my feelings, I realized then that I was supposed to write about butterfly wings. I was supposed to write about change. The dream was given to me as not only a sign for me to prepare, but a sign of what I was supposed to share in this book. The outline for my chapter took shape and I was able to write with ease, all the while knowing she was right there helping me. I was able to place the words into the chapter and create this piece of writing. I am thankful to her for guiding me and helping me write this chapter. Life is full of changes. Some of which we expect to happen: growing older, getting a job, buying a home. Others are not expected: sudden illness, losing a job, the death of a loved one. Many times, and with most changes, we fail to see the actual reason behind them until much further down the road. While in the middle of them, we question if that change is necessary and why the metamorphoses into something different must take place in this way. As we all have, I've had my share of changes come my way so far in my short lifetime. From unexpectedly losing my husband, to having chronic illnesses, watching my children go through hard times, losing my home or vehicles, and so much more. Each time I went through a massive shift of change, I questioned why and I resisted the change in so many ways. Sometimes it was quietly in tears late at night pleading for an answer, and other times in a true temper tantrum style where I was stubborn as heck to accept the change. Each time, I had no idea why the things I deemed unnecessary had to happen in my life. I wondered how life could possibly go on. Each time, I could look back years later and see exactly why it had to happen. I saw all the good things that came from that change, all the butterflies that followed me reminded me daily I was on the right path.

Most people close to me know that when my great-grandmother passed away, I always felt her nearby with yellow butterflies. They seemed to follow me no matter what. It didn't matter the time of year, it seemed they were always fluttering in my path. I always knew she was near and guiding me. Once again, my strong connection to butterflies strongly surfaced in my life as I realized the true meaning of gaining one's wings. She was a magical human being who touched my life in every way possible; she had to let go in order to gain them and be at peace. I knew that the dream about butterflies was meant for way more than a chapter in a book. It showed me that change can be good and not so good. It can even hurt in ways that I cannot imagine. Tears can be shed. Hearts can break. However, when we see through the lenses of change, we see that just like the butterfly has to go through changes to evolve into its beautiful self, the same has to happen in order for us to gain wings and fly to higher places.

The only constant in life is change. Whatever change you just went through, are going through now, or may be about to face, I want you to know that while it is painful, it is also deeply necessary for you to evolve into the beautiful butterfly, to gain your wings, and essential for you to fly. Leaning on that magical assurance can be peaceful in itself when we as humans wish we could figure it out. I can assure you that one day, you will look back and see why the metamorphosis of change had to happen the way it did. You will see the beauty of butterflies, wings, and freedom. Until you can see that reason, you have to lean into the promise that you must go through the lenses of change in order to come out on the other side. If nothing changes, then nothing changes. We do not have to completely understand it at the time.

I still don't fully understand why my beautiful friend had to gain her wings and leave this earth when she did. I feel that as if she had so much left to say and do. However, I know it was necessary for some reason I will not see until I am supposed to see it. Until then, I have to cling to her magic she left here with me and her guidance from above. I have to remind myself to keep her voice alive with words and to keep sharing the magic. I have to remind myself that it was indeed "Written in the Stars" and that she is a true angel that I was blessed to know. She is Magic, YES! Yes, indeed!

Dedicated to my magical sister:

Jennifer M. Kirch

(Nov. 15, 1970 – March 15, 2021)

May you fly high sweet sister and always keep the magic alive.

You will never be forgotten and will always have a voice.

About Blair Hayse:

Blair was born and raised in Tupelo, Mississippi. After graduating high school in 1999 she lived in Birmingham, Alabama before moving back to Mississippi in 2008. She is an avid yoga lover, free spirit, shopping addict and mom to three beautiful children Parker, Millie and Jackson. She is currently residing in Northeast Mississippi and enjoys traveling in her spare time.

Blair has a 19-year background in Corporate America where she worked with billion-dollar companies such has Hilton, Marriott, IHG, Starwood and others. She was called in to create a massive profit in a business so that the company could flip the business or make an investment.

Blair created a legacy in the corporate world where she was sought out for her expertise. The corporate life while exciting and well-paying was exhausting to the single mom of two kids. Blair brought her skills to the online world where she began to help online businesses create a massive flow of profit in a short amount of time. This allowed her the freedom to enjoy her life, travel more and give time to her family.

Blair recently took her interests to her own passion since childhood...writing. She owns Blair Hayse Publishing which offers all-inclusive services to authors to publish their works and create best-selling authors. She offers collaboration books to new authors to build them their own platform. Just this year alone she has helped 83 men and women become best-selling authors. She writes for Thrive Global and Elephant Journal regularly. You can purchase her books on Amazon under her own author page.

Blair currently is a Visibility Strategist Coach, six-time best-selling author and international speaker.. She also offers free resources and paid programs to those interested in building a massive social media platform and becoming an influencer. Recently her company has founded a non-profit sector, RISE Movement, Inc. You can join her FREE Facebook group for some massive value at: Society of Expert to help you increase your visibility.

To connect with Blair:
Email: blairhayseceo@blairhayse.com

Facebook: https://www.facebook.com/blairhayse/

Instagram: https://www.instagram.com/blairhayse/

A Journey of Faith, Self-Reliance, and Perseverance

Karen Quiros

I was 26 and in an aerobics class when I first knew something was wrong. My heart was racing and I felt dizzy. I was working two jobs and biked to and from the gym. I just figured I was tired. My heart returned to normal after I rested. I hopped on my bike and rode home, promising the gym manager that I'd get checked out.

Episodic tachycardia, they called it. When I went to the cardiologist, he found nothing wrong. He suggested that I was drinking too much coffee or diet soda. He said I should eliminate caffeine and come back in a month for a follow-up.

I kept living the same busy overachiever lifestyle, reduced my caffeine intake to the best of my ability, and never experienced tachycardia again. A few weeks later, I was again at the gym when I had another unsettling experience. During the sit-ups portion of a calisthenics class, I noticed that I had intense pain in both my elbows, so much so that I couldn't put my arms up to support my head for a sit-up. A week later, I had a redness in my cheeks and across the bridge of my nose that didn't subside. I started experiencing migrating aches and pains all over my body. Symptoms just kept popping up: back pain, neck pain, hip pain, headaches, hives, fevers; my body was screaming for me to stop and pay attention. I'd take a couple of ibuprofens and keep going, until the fever and pain brought me to the emergency room. They thought I had Lyme disease and prescribed antibiotics. At that time, the testing wasn't the best and treatment was to start a patient on a strong antibiotic. I kept getting sicker. I started having digestive issues, grew weaker, and struggled to keep up with daily life.

I went to my general doctor, who diagnosed me with the trending ailment; back then, it was fibromyalgia. He suggested that I slow down and see a therapist. He gave me prescriptions for muscle relaxers and anti-inflammatories, and said that if those don't help, he would refer me to a rheumatologist. Therapy, muscle relaxers, and anti-inflammatories didn't work, so I found myself at the rheumatologist's office. That's where I learned, after months of blood tests and a skin biopsy, that I had systemic lupus erythematosus. I had never heard of it before. I was told that it was progressive, that there wasn't a cure, and, in my condition, I had five to seven years to live, at best. He said that the best the medical community could do for me was to ease the symptoms. In addition to a long list of medications and follow up appointments, I was referred to physical therapy and a lupus patient support group.

My world came crashing down. I felt miserable, lost, and very alone. The doctors told me that death was imminent, and gave my life an expiration date when I was only 26 years old. I had dreams of meeting my knight in shining armor, having the house with a white picket fence, a dog, and home filled with children. Hearing this diagnosis made me angry and violated my beliefs. After a few months of following doctor's orders, none of which were helping me, I decided to abandon their methods and find a way to cure myself of this disease. I had overcome anorexia and bulimia; I would overcome this, too! I could not and would not live in misery or accept that I was going to die in my 30s.

On my next visit to the rheumatologist, I shared my decision to heal my body naturally. He told me that I was making a very big mistake and warned me that they wouldn't be able to help me if I took herbal remedies, because his team wasn't trained in them. He continued to caution me that if I didn't follow their protocol, I'd lose the battle sooner. I thought to myself, "No I won't, but I will if I keep taking pharmaceutical medications!" He proceeded to paint a picture of what death would look like when my kidneys failed. He said I was in denial and should see a therapist, that I needed emotional support. I had already made my decision and wasn't going to let his words of discouragement and fear change my plan.

I'd ask myself, "Why would I want to continue taking medications that exhausted and fattened me, changed my personality, and intoxicated my body?" In my opinion, the medications were going to destroy my kidneys and self-esteem long before lupus would. The doctors gave me no hope, just a grim outlook. I questioned why I would want to continue down a path of gloom and doom when I had the option of possibility and exploration. What if? What if I could cure this disease? In my opinion, the medical system had already failed me, so I forged ahead, alone. I trusted my decision to heal myself naturally. It became my life's mission as I held the faith and the vision of my long, healthy life. I fought a good fight and won.

Now that I made the decision to move away from traditional Western medicine, I had to prove that I made the right choice. My young spirit was speaking and it refused to accept that the doctors might be right. I thought to myself, "I have a lot of life to live. My life is precious. I see a long, healthy future and I want a second chance!" In the back of my mind, I wondered if lupus was a punishment for not loving myself enough and honoring the magnificent body that God had given me. As if having anorexia and bulimia for four years wasn't enough of a punishment.

I prayed for guidance. How will I heal my body? Where do I start? My soul's wisdom and the angels guided me *every* step of the way. Sometimes I listened, and sometimes I didn't. At times, I'd get tired, frustrated, discouraged, and disappointed, especially when I was dutifully committed to a healthy lifestyle and my health regressed for no apparent reason. I eventually figured out that each time I had a setback, I had ventured back to that overachiever lifestyle I had been living. My impatience and anger sometimes got the better of me, testing my faith time and time again. I'd have a pity party, then put my big girl pants back on and forge ahead. I fought to stay the course of the road less traveled. The sweet guidance of my soul wasn't ever going to let me down, and I wasn't about to disappoint. My lupus healing journey was an exercise of faith in my soul's guidance. Learning to listen to and heed my soul's wisdom took time to hone.

The Beginning of My Healing Journey

The first step in my journey was to learn all that I could about lupus and its effects on the body. I remembered every word I read and envisioned what my body might be looking like inside when it was inflamed. I asked my body what it needed, and waited for the answers. 34 years ago, we didn't have the internet, so the library became my reliable source of information to begin my healing journey. There were only a couple of books available on lupus, none of which gave me any hope of healing. They described how to manage the symptoms and plan for a debilitating future and timely death.

I had a past of bulimia and anorexia, so I decided to focus on studying nutrition. My body was probably depleted of nutrients, which may have contributed to developing this disease. I enrolled in college and devoured every book I could find on biochemistry and nutrition. There was a plethora of information, but only a limited selection of research-based publications regarding the relationship between diet and an autoimmune disease; there were many theories that had differing views about nutrition. My biggest takeaway was that there was no one "diet fits all" when it comes to healing. If I wanted to heal, I had to intently listen to my body...but how would I do that? What did my body need to heal?

I rented every meditation cassette tape that the library had. I listened to them every day until I developed my own daily visualization practice. Meditation and breath work became my medication. I started each meditation with the intention of learning what my body needed from me that day, and then visualized divine healing taking place. Lupus was my teacher, and faith my guide.

I was guided to question and research everything, leaving no stone unturned. I believed that anything could have triggered the deterioration of my immune system. I knew that if I could restore it, it would function optimally again. I was steadfast in my belief that I could heal myself, and the energy of my belief fueled my healing. There were setbacks and suffering, but my faith never wavered.

It took me time, but I learned to fully trust my soul's guidance. I was guided through every step of my healing, and focused on every level of my being: my faith, self-care, self-love, self-commitment, self-esteem, and the practice of forgiveness, surrender, and never giving up hope. I changed my diet, I healed my gut from the ravages of antibiotics, and nurtured my body with clean water, air, and environment. I learned about how harmful electromagnetic fields and geopathic stress are on the immune system. I discovered how our beliefs create our reality. I studied energy medicine and the work of Royal Raymond Rife, Dr. Valerie Hunt, and Dr. Hulda Clark. I understood how taking medications could further intoxicate an already toxic and weakened body. I learned the healing benefits of grounding in nature, and the pain relieving, restorative effects of the ocean. I allowed the sunshine to caress my body, in spite of the fact that I was told to stay out of the sun. I tuned into my soul every single day, sometimes more than once. I journaled and followed the direction of my soul, my God source, and healed my body from the effects of lupus.

Today, and for the past 26 plus years, I live lupus free. I am healed.

I say 26 *plus* years because I healed prior to 1994, which is the year I gave birth to my first child. I had five tubal pregnancies before that, but that's for another chapter! Prior to attempting to get pregnant via IVF intervention, my OB/GYN was concerned that pregnancy would exacerbate the disease, and, in doctors' words, I'd no longer be in remission. I respected, but graciously denied their belief, although I was questioned and cautioned during my visits. After giving birth, the doctors said that I was lucky, but shouldn't consider getting pregnant again because I might not be lucky a second time. They said I should be appreciative, and, since I had a child to care for now, it would be irresponsible of me to attempt getting pregnant again. I struggled with various health challenges in the years following as a result of endometriosis and multiple surgeries, but I healed from those as well. Eventually, I had another beautiful child.

My story of healing from lupus is one of faith and learning how to listen to my soul's guidance. No matter what health challenges I've been labeled with over my lifetime, I've sent a clear message to my body that I'm not going to live my life identifying with a diagnosis. A diagnosis is only a name given to a set of symptoms; it is not my destiny. I'm going to find a way to heal.

God created all of us to be self-reliant and gave us the ability to heal ourselves. I also believe that our fabulous medical system is in place for emergencies, and not as a go-to for all health ailments. We must learn to trust our inner guidance, for it is where we discover what we need to heal ourselves. As soon as we seek healing outside of ourselves, we give our healing over to someone else. In essence, we're telling ourselves that we don't trust our own guidance, our God self. Just as no two people have the same fingerprints, no two people require the exact healing path.

Believe in yourself. When you believe you can, you will. Your beliefs become your reality. If you believe you are sick, you stay sick. If you believe you are healthy, you will heal. I know it's not an easy road, but your life is worth believing in and fighting for. Faith, belief, and disciplined action facilitate healing.

If you're suffering with an ailment, here's the affirmation I used to help me heal. Change it to honor your soul: Thank you, God, for this body of perfection. I promise to tune in and listen to my soul and follow its wisdom to keep it healthy and strong. I am healthy, I am healed, I am whole.

About Karen Quiros:

Karen was born and raised on Long Island, New York. She has been married to her soulmate for 27 years and counting, and has two sons who she calls her beautiful blessings. Karen is a homesteader at heart and loves gardening, being a chicken mama, and beekeeper. She enjoys spending time with her family and friends, researching, traveling, baking, knitting, cycling, yoga, and spending time in nature.

Karen has run the wellness practice, Balanced Wellness Consulting, since 2001. This is where she guides and supports clients desiring to heal themselves naturally using her experience and training as a nurse, craniosacral therapist, nutritionist, Reiki Master, quantum biofeedback specialist, and sound healer, along with meditation and yoga.

She balances her time between Long Island and Costa Rica, where she facilitates workshops and soul-nourishing retreats using her signature program the Happiness Compass©, along with Chakradance® and SoulCollage©. Karen created the Happiness Compass© to be a life-changing online workshop that teaches women how to connect with the wisdom of their Soul for guidance to create a healthy, joy-filled, deeply fulfilling life.

Since healing herself from lupus, Karen has dedicated her life to learning all she can about the marvels of natural healing, energy medicine, and spirituality. She is passionate about helping women heal themselves and teaching them how to listen to their soul for wisdom and lifelong guidance. Keep an eye out for her upcoming book *Lupus: Starving the Wolf* in late 2021 where she details her lupus-healing journey.

To connect with Karen:

Email: karen@balwell.com

Facebook: https://www.facebook.com/karenmayquiros

Facebook Group "Women Creating a Happier World":
www.facebook.com/groups/womencreatingahappierworld

Website: www.balwell.com

Happiness Compass© Online Workshop:
https://balancedwellness.clickfunnels.com/program

The Purr Effect

Brooke J. Coleman

"Sexuality is one of the ways that we become enlightened, actually,
because it leads us to self-knowledge." -Alice Walker
sex-u-al-i-ty /sekSHo͞oˈalədē/
noun
1. capacity for sexual feelings.

"she began to understand the power of her sexuality"
Oxford Languages

What does it feel like to put yourself first? What does this process look like for you? What does it feel like to be in your own skin? What does it look like to be in tune with your sexuality? These are all questions I have found myself struggling with as a young woman. I did not really think about the importance of any of these questions and how they would gain significance in my adulthood until after I begin my journey of studying to become a certified sexologist.

Through this journey, I began to learn that faking orgasms, being voiceless in the bedroom, and having bad sex is a waste of energy. Instead, I needed to get a real view of what sexual pleasure looked like for me. It was time for me to embrace my sexuality and accept myself as a sexual being. See, that's the thing, mostly everyone resonates with being a human being, but do people resonate with being a sexual being? It is 2021 and I still see people cringe when they hear the word "sex." It makes them uncomfortable because it is still viewed as a taboo subject. Even today, sex is still not a dinner table type of conversation. Sex brings back memories, whether they are good or not so good ones. It makes you feel hot and kind of squeamish at the same time. How dare she talk about sex and all those secular things in front of us "saved" folks? How dare she own her sexuality? How dare she walk around with confidence thinking that she can just ask for what she wants?

Contrary to what you may have been taught, exploring your sexuality is key to tapping into your own divine power. It means that you are continually choosing to seek out the knowledge of your own unique preferences and personal desires. It means that you are making a choice to discover your body and your wishes by listening to your sexual intuition. It is important to be clear on what your limited beliefs are around your own sexuality so you can begin to explore these limits with love. Culturally, as women, we have developed a generational pattern of being seen and not heard, being programmed to be grateful for what we have, and to not steer too far into our individuality. We are kept under this societal nametag and "moral" standards of the qualities of who a woman should be.

My personal journey with sex started late in high school. Before I met "the guy," I never really thought much about sex. Of course, I had been hearing about sex since my middle school years. Some of my friends at school had already experienced this thing called sex. They gave their opinions about it but hadn't dove into the deep waters just yet. Most of my sexual knowledge as a teenager came from stories that my classmates shared about their sexual escapades and from a group of virgins who freely gave their opinions about activities that they had not even tested out yet. The tools that I was equipped with as a teenager were not much, but gave me ideas and the answer that I, personally, was not ready to explore sex.

I was the baby girl of my family. I had older sisters in high school and they had boyfriends, but I was truly never the girl that felt she needed a title or a boy to make her happy. A lot of guys at my middle school were immature, so it was easy for me to not think about sex. I barely thought about boys as "boyfriend material," much less in a sexual way. I didn't have my first "real" boyfriend until eighth grade, or at least the first boy that I allowed to publicly "claim" me with a title. He was nice, cute, and funny, but I never really looked at him in a sexual tone.

Back in the 90s, kissing was where it was at! I was having a blast in that lane. Enjoying the thought of sweet kisses by the lockers was everything to me at that time. I was not ready for all that extra "sex stuff" no matter how many of my friends were participating. In middle school, the highlights of my relationship were being walked to class while we held hands, stealing a kiss after the bell rang for school to let out, and rushing home after practice to grab my light-up phone to hear his voice before curfew. Those were the days! However, the poems, letters, and sexual suggestions began a few months into the relationship. Don't get me wrong, I really liked him. His poems were cool, but I didn't feel like making the next move with him. Hell, what did I even know about sex? I was only 13.

At that time, I could not even remember having a sex talk with my parents. Although the movies will have you believe that every family has "the birds and the bees" conversation with their children, I cannot recall a time it was held with me or my sisters. There was maybe a touch here or there over time in an educational way, as my mom has a background in education, but not one of enough depth for use in my adult life or to pass onto my children. I now have two girls that I am raising to be young women, and I will eventually have to have this "sex talk" with all three of my children. I did not realize that the lack of sexual knowledge when I was younger would give me a lack of sexual confidence as a grown woman.

In the 10th grade, I lost my virginity to my now husband. Although, I do not like to use the word "lost" when I speak about virginity because it is nothing that a girl loses. It should be looked at as something that a girl chooses to share with the person she chooses. I think that is another misconception when it comes to a young girl's first experience with sex, sexuality, and the social mindset we have behind these taboo acts. My first experiences with sex were truly divine. My boyfriend took care of me, shared his love with me, took his time, and honored my body and my space; he did everything that I thought should be experienced during sex. It was perfect. These are memories that I still hold in my heart today.

After high school, I went off to college and was engaged to my high school sweetheart a few years later. We went on to get married and have three beautiful children. Sex was still great, and I adored being able to please my partner. However, about seven years into my marriage, even though my husband and I continued to do the same things we enjoyed and he still made me feel the same way as I did in high school, I felt unfulfilled deep down. Something inside of me still felt lost when it came to the limited knowledge I had of sex. I still did not know much about sex besides the sex I was having in my marriage, the sex that I had experienced throughout my high school and college years with my partner, the sex I had seen in porn, and the sex that I had heard other grown folks talking about at social events. I asked myself, *Am I even having sex correctly?*

I was a 28-year-old woman still learning about my sexuality and how to be comfortable with being a sexual being. I still did not know much about my own body and how it worked, so it was easier for me to allow myself to focus more on giving my partner pleasure rather than worry about receiving my own pleasure. Somehow, not fulfilling my own pleasure left a void inside me. Being afraid of speaking out on what I desired sexually kept me from vibrating higher. Not owning my sexuality nor finding the courage to ask for the things that I desired left me feeling a lack of confidence in other areas of my life. How can I have the courage to go after the job I really want if I cannot even ask my partner to have the type of intimate connection with me that I now desire?

I was terrified to suggest trying and experiencing something different with me sexually, terrified my partner would look at me weird as if it changed who I was or who my partner expected me to be. My biggest fear of asking for new things was his reaction. How would I be judged? What if my partner thinks that I have tried these acts somewhere else and now I want to bring them home? What makes me want to try these new things now at this point in my life? What is wrong with the way I have been doing things? Why the sudden change now, and are you trying to say that the things you have are not enough for you? Having this list of concerns on my mind, even though I have not even had the conversation yet, made me sweat. I was setting myself up for failure before I gave it a real effort.

I allowed myself to stay in the shadows because I was not comfortable in my own skin as a sexual being. I was afraid to own my sexuality as a woman. I didn't take ownership over something that is a natural part of me, and it dimmed my light in other areas of my life. I carried this lack of confidence in every part of my life. It was not until I began to discover my own body and really tap into my own sexual intuition through the art of self-exploration that I was able to really connect with my truth.

I was so wrapped up in my societal nametag. I was happy with being of service to my family, and at that time in my life, I did not see myself as a people pleaser but as someone who was simply doing what I felt came naturally to me as a woman. Around the eighth year of my marriage and after having our third child, I became a consultant for an adult intimacy line so I could stay home and work. I really enjoyed educating women about their bodies and owning their sexuality through the toy parties I hosted for them in their homes. After two years, I decided to go back to school to become a certified sex and relationship coach.

Throughout my education journey, I was still nervous. I did not want my partner to be intimidated by my new knowledge or look at me differently after all these years, but I felt a craving to own my sexuality. I learned some fascinating things about myself during this journey. I was finally gaining knowledge about my body that I felt I did not receive as a young woman. I was growing more comfortable in my own skin and as a sexual being with this new awareness. When I began to practice what I was preaching, my mind expanded. As I took more time to explore myself in ways that were pleasing to me, I climbed to a higher dimension and was enlightened to my own understanding of what pleasure feels like to me. I began to evolve instead of repeat. I released the stigmas and traumas I held behind sex, and my experiences with sex changed. I opened my heart to receive all the love I had to give myself. I knew that I was worthy of having all the pleasure I desired in my life.

Once I began to connect with my own sexuality and sexual identity, my sex life changed forever. See, it was not that I was having bad sex, I just didn't have the right mindset about sex. Although I did not particularly know what kind of pleasure I wanted, I was excited about this new voyage at 35 years old. I could not remember a time when I was truly having sex for myself before this journey. I was present and it was of my free will, but I don't think I was truly having sex for my own pleasure.

If asked to recall an open conversation that I have shared with a woman or a group of women about what owning their pleasure looks like, I would have no references. While women are quick to share their recipes and parenting tips with other women, they are not so quick to share their intimate stories. As I took more time to explore myself, sex became more desirable. I experienced a freedom of sexual expression, and discovered that I could share these experiences as "table talk" with friends. There is something amazing about knowing what your body truly desires. It is like having a map to this beautiful, unforeseen location full of hidden treasures, written in a language that only you speak, and therefore only you know how to guide your ship. to the secrecy.

Knowing yourself entirely is immensely powerful. I became confident in my truth and gained a newfound strength in my abilities. I found my voice so that when I speak, I can do so with bravery and self-assurance. I began to show up in the world in a more authentic way, now having the knowledge of self-awareness created new experiences in my life. Through the practice of self-exploration, I have been able to manifest my greatest desires. We all have the power of creation inside of us, and that is the Purr Effect. Every woman has that power; the question is, will you have the courage to channel it?

"If sexuality is one dimension of our ability to live passionately in the world then in cutting off our sexual feelings we diminish our overall power to feel, know, and value deeply." -Judith Plaskow

About Brooke J. Coleman:

Brooke Coleman is a Texas native. She was born and raised in the small town of Port Arthur where she was a part of the first graduating class of Memorial High School in 2003. Afterwards, she began her studies at Texas Southern University and went on to snag her Master's in Education in June 2012.

After graduating from college, Brooke began her journey in the education field. She proudly mentored dozens of elementary, middle, and high school students along the way, but still felt something was missing somehow. She desired to make a greater impact on the world, but was not sure how she would accomplish it. Brooke had the passion to uplift, inspire, and educate young women in a more authentic way. She was sparked to start a new journey, which led to her studying sexology and spiritual healing as a way to help bridge the gap between sexuality and spirituality.

Brooke knew that it was vital to share this knowledge with people all over the world. She wanted to help people learn how to be comfortable with who they are as spiritual and sexual beings while removing the shame that society imposes on sexuality. These days, Brooke enjoys sharing these teachings on her weekly podcast, digital workshops, intimate events, and group coaching programs. Although she still considers herself to be a small-town country gal from Port Arthur, Brooke is overjoyed to be able to share her magic with people all over the globe.

Brooke is a crystal loving, moon watching free spirit and mother of three beautiful children: Jania, Royal, and Taylor. She currently resides in southeast Texas and enjoys volunteering and traveling in her spare time.

To connect with Brooke:

Email: http://theepleasureboss@gmail.com

Gumroad: https://gumroad.com/thepleasureboss

Instagram: https://www.instagram.com/thepleasureboss/

Linktree: https://linktr.ee/thepleasureboss

Grit

Mistie S. Rose

I've heard it said that not everything you lose is actually a loss. It took me about a decade to really process those words appropriately. Several years ago, when my daughter lost her father, I'm not sure what was actually lost that day. He was 28 years old and his organs helped save at least four lives. Hope was gained for many waiting on a kidney, a liver, a lung…but I felt numb. A feeling of surprise overtook me. Disbelief, really.

A little more than a decade ago, I was married to my first husband. He was stationed at Seymour Johnson Air Force Base in Goldsboro, North Carolina. Upon our arrival, I accepted my first job at the Army and Air Force Exchange Service, a store with a little bit of everything in it. I was 23 years old at the time and a new cashier. It was just the two of us in our early 20s, no thoughts of savings or retirement. I looked at it like an easy job that kept me busy while my husband was away.

After about three deployments, my marriage fell apart and we decided to separate. We had grown into different people during all that time apart. Feeling sorry for myself, I went out to karaoke with co-workers that had become my good friends. It was not an unusual Friday night, as we did this often, but I generally drank less than I did on this particular evening. I ended up going home with a friend, or someone I thought was a friend.

A couple of months later, I came home for lunch and grabbed one of the four half-gallons of orange juice out of my fridge. I didn't even bother to grab a glass and drank it right out of the carton. I took a jar of pizza sauce out of the pantry, looked for the largest spoon I had, and sat on the ground to rest my legs, which were more tired than usual. As I sat there, chugging orange juice and eating pizza sauce straight from the jar, it dawned on me that something might be off. I made an appointment with my doctor, and about a week later, I found out I was pregnant.

I was not thrilled about the prospect of being a newly separated pregnant lady, yet the ideas of adoption or abortion were the furthest from my mind. I just knew this happened to me for a reason, the reason being because I had been stupid and irresponsible. I had never wanted children and hadn't spent much time thinking about it. Now that it was here, I knew I needed to follow through with it.

Not knowing what to do next and with no support in North Carolina, I moved home to Boise, Idaho and back into my old high school bedroom. My parents, who know me well, also knew that I had been stupid and irresponsible. They let me come home to have the baby, and I felt like I was 16 and pregnant the whole time. I had no idea what to do and looked to my doctors and mother to tell me what I should be doing completely.

In October 2009, I had a healthy, tiny, five-pound and six-ounce baby girl. That day, the world stopped revolving around me. I loved this baby with a depth I hadn't even known was possible. She became everything that meant anything to me. Unfortunately, this was a far cry from what her father felt. He essentially said, "No, thanks." From that day forward, he never took an ounce of responsibility for creating a life.

When my daughter was about two years old, my mom helped me file court documents to get full physical and legal custody. It was uncontested. We asked that the father start paying child support. In North Carolina, child support is a percentage of what you make, not what you could make working a full-time minimum wage job as is the law in Idaho. He was ordered to pay 50 dollars a month and failed to even do that. Yet, my daughter never had a second thought about not having a mother and father; she had a mother and a grandmother. She thought this situation was very normal and all she needed.

Years later, her father died. I was notified by his mother. She asked me to come say goodbye to him and that she'd keep him on life support until I got there. I declined her offer. I hadn't seen or heard from this person in a number of years and didn't feel the loss like his mother did. In fact, I didn't feel a loss at all. I had been raising his child without him for years. Of course, I missed out on sharing the knowledge that someone else cares as much as you do about the little accomplishments and milestones a baby makes daily. These were things my friends had with their husbands and I did not; I only had my mom to share that with. My brothers and other family shared them as well, but I knew it wasn't as monumental to them as it was to me. I did not miss the financial support or the partnership, I missed having another care for her the amount that I did. Her father couldn't have been farther from that person.

After his death, I experienced a variety of emotions, the most prominent being anger. I had always clung to the idea that one day, he would have to answer to her. He would have to look our daughter in the eye and explain himself, his absence, and come up with some reason for all of it, because he had never given me one. I figured he owed her at least that. One day when she is older, she may want to explore learning about who her father was and why he was resoundingly absent. Everything drove me mad, from every injustice that happened to every sleepless night I had that he hadn't. I really thought that one day, he would have to tell her. In dying, it was just another thing he got out of: he will never have to explain himself, and neither my daughter nor I will ever know why he didn't choose her for all these years. If anything, she deserves an explanation.

The tears I shed over him were out of anger and not sadness. I always felt it to be so unfair. My mother would snap back at me, "Life is not fair, a fair is a place you go to have fun." This, I assume, is either her way of comforting me or telling me to toughen up. The anger almost consumed me in the weeks following his death. This injustice and that I could do nothing about it ate me up. What had my sweet daughter done to deserve such a selfish person in her life? Now, she would never even hear an apology from him, an apology that is so well-deserved.

I started to realize I needed to talk about it to someone. I started with my friends, my mother, and ended up in traditional talk therapy. Perhaps I needed to vent, to really be heard, or to have another verify that the events that had unfolded were in fact unfair. I needed to know I wasn't crazy and that my expectations weren't too high. Validation, that is what I went looking for. I still ended up angry for a long time. Many months were spent angry mixed with self-pity and disdain for the fact that I too contributed to this outcome by going home with this "friend."

Eventually, I had to dig deep past the anger and look at the dirty, gritty root causes of the emotion in order to get past it. I began to take responsibility for my own actions and choices that had led me to where I was. It took me a while to really accept them. Once I began this process, I started to make room in my heart for emotions other than anger and injustice. This began to snowball into forgiveness and even gratitude. Without her father, I wouldn't have the most precious treasure in my life: my daughter.

Throughout my journey, I've learned a lot about therapy. Talk therapy usually focuses on minimizing symptoms and creating solutions. It may be more beneficial to ensure it is not seen as a whole life fix and rather an intervention in a mental health issue. Managing expectations is crucial, and knowing that the work one puts in is in turn the benefit one gets out. Another thing to think about is the continuous management and cultivation of an open-ended timeline of our progress in talk therapy. This process can sometimes take longer than we anticipate, but can lead to some of the most wonderful results. Having trouble with daily activities, problems with adjusting to aspects of life, along with dealing with issues from trauma, or experiencing grief are just some of the reasons people seek therapy. There are many different obstacles that therapists can help you overcome, as well as different approaches that a well-trained therapist will try to help you address in a safe way that is easy for you to process. Traditional talk therapy also can have a fairly high drop-out rate, but what help do we get if we quit trying? In my journey of talk therapy over the years, I have encountered all of these issues.

The therapist I had was wonderful. In the beginning of my talk therapy journey, I would see her twice a week. When my baby was not sleeping and my mom was working, sometimes my therapist would be the most interaction I would have with another adult. The way she walked me through my issues, validated my feelings, and made me feel truly heard was incredible. While there are lots of other therapies, talk therapy can be a good option when undergoing stress, you just can't seem to get out from under. I would recommend this type of self-help to anyone. I learned I had feelings on a broader scale than I had ever known.

My therapist helped me to find solutions. She asked me open-ended "What if?" questions to which I never had the wrong answer. I stopped being worried about being wrong when I knew I was in a safe space where my thoughts and feelings were all okay to have, no matter what they were. As long as a person isn't a danger to themselves or others, all of the things spoken in therapy remain completely private. The benefits for me were tremendous and the validation priceless. I generally feel less anxiety and depression since starting therapy. Sometimes I would have complete elimination of symptoms, while other times I learned how to better control them.

Coming from a position of experience, I would encourage anyone to make a positive life change and seek whatever therapy is the best fit for their problem. Gaining control feels weightless, and finding out that my emotions are mine to control was quite a freeing lesson. No one can "make me" angry or sad without me allowing it to happen. I choose the emotion; thus, control how I respond to stressors and triggers. I no longer see a therapist, but the tools I have gained spending time in therapy are irreplaceable. They have certainly helped me to be a better parent and live a life far happier than I had ever imagined. Worry grows in our minds if that's what it's focused on, but so does love, joy, and happiness. It's up to us to simply choose it.

About Mistie S. Rose:

Mistie Rose became a #1 International Bestselling author in December 2020 as a contributing author in *She is Magic, Always*. While she loves to write, her real passion is in community health. She has obtained both undergraduate and graduate degrees in Public Health at Boise State University. She has over 10 years of experience working in the healthcare field.

Mistie loves living in beautiful Boise, Idaho with her darling husband, daughter, and stepson. Her family has a lovely home in the Boise foothills where she enjoys hiking the hills and biking. She also volunteers through Happy Jack Cats, Inc to take care of local foster kitties. Her family jokes about starting their own zoo as they have adopted three perfect cats and two cute canines.

To connect with Mistie:

Facebook: https://www.facebook.com/mistie.rose.7

Instagram: https://www.instagram.com/mistienellie/
Photo Credit: Danielle Vanderwiel Photography

Head Full of Flowers

Kelsey Rojas

Goodbye

I'm in this moment-
feeling my heart break for the first time.
So deeply in my gut,
I can tell-
I'll never be the same

If you're wondering how I knew it was over, it was your eyes. They used to drip honey gold for me, but now I don't think you even see me anymore. It was also your lips- when you kissed me hello, I swear I could already taste the goodbye.

Toxic

I wanted him to love me so much-
I stopped loving myself.

And I think he loved that most of all.

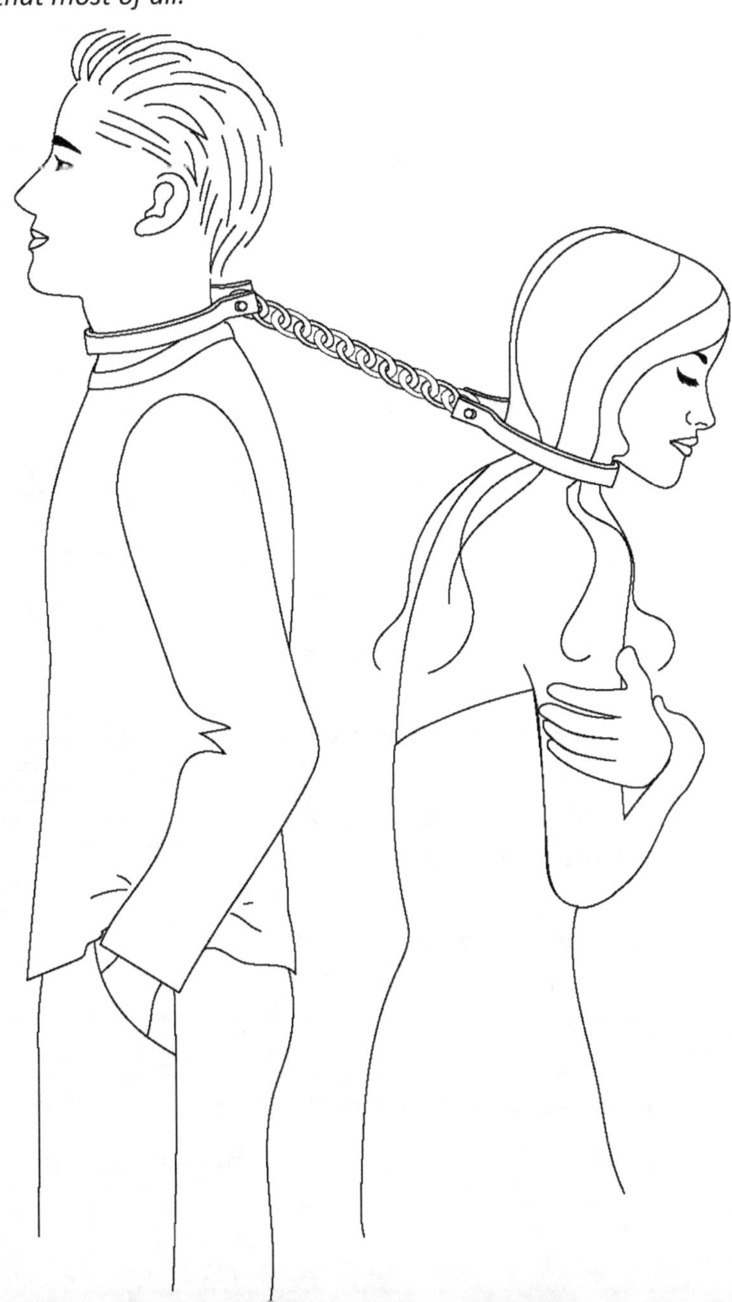

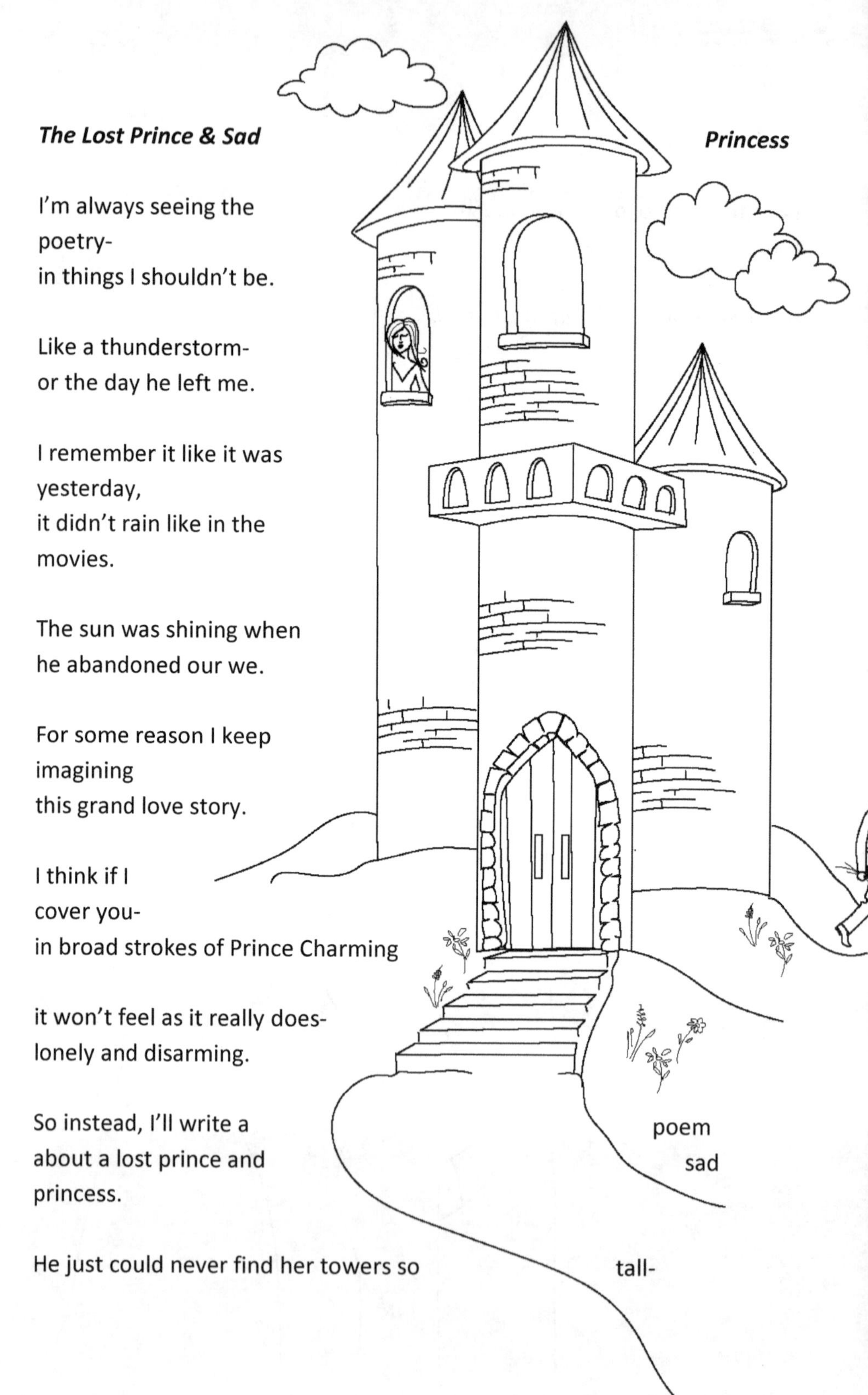

The Lost Prince & Sad **Princess**

I'm always seeing the
poetry-
in things I shouldn't be.

Like a thunderstorm-
or the day he left me.

I remember it like it was
yesterday,
it didn't rain like in the
movies.

The sun was shining when
he abandoned our we.

For some reason I keep
imagining
this grand love story.

I think if I
cover you-
in broad strokes of Prince Charming

it won't feel as it really does-
lonely and disarming.

So instead, I'll write a
about a lost prince and
princess.

He just could never find her towers so

each day he searched less and less.

What a much better tale-
a story worth reading before the children have slept.

But the truth is they shared a love,
unworthy of being kept.

The Insufficiencies of Love

The poison leaked from his lips
and flourished my soul-
he said it was love this
time.

So, I allowed his
hands to graze my
skin-
like lightning
striking the sand.

He made love hurt more
but saw me like vibrant glass-
one he could easily shatter.

The thing about fragile things-
they always trust the wrong
hands.

Much too concerned with being
held,
I never worried much about
being kept.
So, I wasn't surprised when he took
my thunder away.

The sunshine still hasn't come back,
but I see you so much more clearly now.

Love would never be enough.
He knew I was meant for the sun-
I'd never find safety in his storm.

The Kind of Love That Goes Away

Growing Up

I wanted to love him,
he reminded me
of cool summer evenings-
mistakes made in clouded rooms.

I needed to love him,
he told me
that I was a fiery
sunset-
he was obsessed
with my brightness.

I wanted love,
I was alone for
so long
with no real end
in sight-
who was I without the
love of a man?

I needed love,
I keep thinking about
everything,
I'm dying to feel fireworks-
all I feel is this loneliness.

I want-
well to be honest,
I don't know what I
I keep searching for
other people's arms.

I need-
to wrap myself
in the love I'm dreaming of,
I want to be my own soulmate.

I think they call this growth.

Writer's Block

I keep wandering around my mind,
looking for flowers and words to combine-
but instead, I keep bumping into you.
You're around every corner,
holding a bouquet of dead peonies,
reminding me that you poisoned my garden long ago-
a daisy hasn't bloomed in years.
Sometimes pain gives you poetry,
other times it gives you pages
of half-written, lonely prose.

The wreckage you left behind has my   *poetry caught in thick*
vines, with thorns entangling my   *words in doubt and*
fear. But the fields of flowers are   *becoming wilder as*
my heart heals- a strength I never   *had coming out*
of me. You've
controlled my
poetry for   *too*
long,   *and*
now my
hands will tell
the truth I've
been too scared to
share.

Starting Over

Starting over isn't easy,
I guess no one ever made
think it would be.

The ease of it admittedly
was so far from my mind-
all I saw was open road.

When you're so focused,
on the way out,
you don't consider what you've left.

Starting over in my new
I left some of my old
scars-
just so when I look
the mirror,
I still remember
her.

The girl I
was so
desperate
to outrun-
she's so
lonely
now.
The
comfortability
of my darkness

used to keep us warm at night.

I know the choices I made are right-
and I know I'm not the girl you usually have to check on.
I'm the one dead set on brighter and lovelier.

But I'm also the one
pushing away the pain,
picking myself off the floor-
trying to remember my worth.

To be honest,
beginning again
sometimes feels a lot like running-
and I'm so fucking tired.

Sometimes I wish I was the victim of my own story. Being the hero is so exhausting, there's never anyone to save me.

You Used Me

You used me-
you wanted to feel magic,
so, you thought holding the
of a poet would give that to

You used me-
someone once told you
that you were unlovable.
So, you wanted me to
and sunshine soaked

I can tell now
that you used me.
You took the thing that
and turned it on me.
You're still doing it now-
my hands can't help but keep
writing you into existence.

Your narcissism means
you love to see your effect on me.
How you went ahead,
ripped my poetry apart,
and left me bleeding next to
the black ink.

But since you used me,
I have found that my
words
demand

on my behalf,
fighting my war of heartbreak-
since you left me weak and empty.

So yes, you used me-
but maybe I used you a little, too.
Because the poetry is pouring out of me-
telling stories about a boy
who wanted to ruin me.
But darling, I turned this pain into gold-
try and use me now.

A Head Full of Flowers

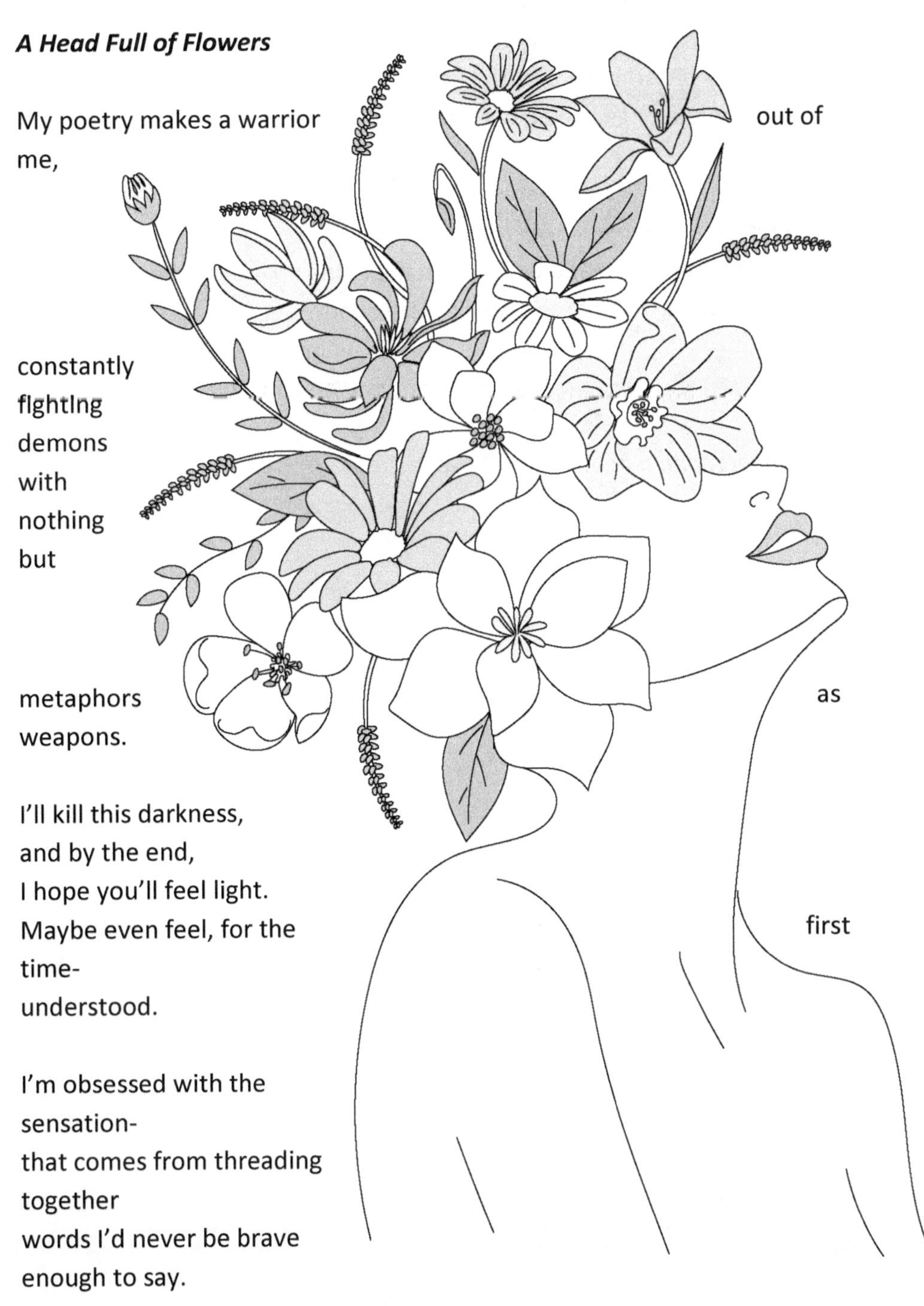

My poetry makes a warrior
me,

out of

constantly
fighting
demons
with
nothing
but

metaphors
weapons.

as

I'll kill this darkness,
and by the end,
I hope you'll feel light.
Maybe even feel, for the
time-
understood.

first

I'm obsessed with the
sensation-
that comes from threading
together
words I'd never be brave
enough to say.

It makes me forget the fire they were birthed in.

The pain is so bitter in my mouth like bile,
but sweet on the page like an old friend.

My poetry makes my heartache so beautiful-
I find myself falling in love with the scars.
For the first time I've made peace with the pain-
a strength coming out of me I never knew I had.

"What makes you think you can write your pain away, what makes you so worthy?"
A pen, paper, and a head full of flowers.

Inner Peace

You can feel her now-
the girl who shut out her own heart.
Her energy is holding hands
walking beside you-
she's a friend again.
She lost herself
her absence
by all

love
But now, you
her again.
An aura glowing from
her own inner peace.
A light shining so
bright,
you won't lose her
again.

For the first time in so long, my heart is open. I made a nasty habit of hiding away my genuine self. I wanted so badly to be liked and worried little about what I loved. Now, my arms are open wide, and I want to embrace the gift of opportunity. I deserve this chance.

I was once a fragile bird with a broken wing, so scared of the open air, but still desperately longed to be reunited with the clouds. I've wasted so much time wishing to be able to fly again, and now it's time to push myself out of my safe nest. I've healed, and it's my turn to soar.

You Deserve to Love Yourself First

You took root inside me,
planted yourself sweetly by the daisies.
Watered your roses everyday-
checked to make sure they grew.

With a garden so
roses growing up
blooming out of
all I could see

beautiful,
through my throat,
my eyes,
was you.

It wasn't for
until I started to feel
drowning from the
blood drawn
by your roses-
thorns lacerating my
throat.

months,
my daisies dying,

You rooted yourself inside me,
disguised so sweetly-
flowers with the promise of love.
Instead, all I feel is the pain.

You're gone now,
your garden has finally died-
no more roses, no more you.

I never thought I'd try again,
to build a garden.
I settled for the barren wasteland
you left behind

Until I met him-
with his green thumb and hazel eyes,
restoring my world with light-
giving me life.

He took my hand and placed seeds
meant for daisies, and he smiled-
the kind of smile that could make
wildflowers grow in hell.

"Don't you want to plant your sunflowers?" I cried.
"Why are you giving me daises? I thought you loved me."
I'll never forget what he said-
I carry it every day,
every time I look at our kitchen table-
filled with a beautiful bouquet.

*"You need to plant this daisy in your heart before I can give you
sunflowers. You deserve to love yourself first."*

Timing Is Everything

I used to lay in my bed,
and imagine him   beside me.
What   would he look like?
What   would he feel like?

And as I got   older,
I tried to fill
that place-
a different man
lying beside me,
whispering his
sweet
nothings.

The
desperate
search for you
led me to the darkest
places
my life had ever known.
I kept thinking-
was love supposed to feel this way?

And when you found me,
I had stopped daydreaming-
about how you might kiss my forehead,
or what we'd laugh about.

It was when I gave up
on the search for Mr. Right,
did the universe, open up her arms-
smile at me and say, *"You're ready."*

And there you were-
standing over six feet tall.
A pair of hazel eyes,
my new favorite color.

Moving On

It is both sad and wonderful
that I no longer miss you.

Your lips aren't imprinted on my skin anymore-
his lips are all I can taste now.

I have forgotten how it sounds when you laugh,
or the jokes you used to say.

My heart doesn't belong to you anymore-
I gathered the strength to give it to someone better.

I

shouldn't be sorry
for letting go of you.

Especially since-
you gave up on me first.

But some part of me will always be nostalgic
for the boy with the scratchy beard and funny smile.

I adore him-
he is not you.

And that is both sad,
and wonderful.

Rose-Colored Glasses

Like a life of darkness lifted,
there the world shined.
So bright to me-
like I'd opened my eyes for the first time.
And maybe I had,
I've always been so tired-
but here,
with you-
I'm awakened by hope.

It's as if I've never known sunlight before. I don't remember not only seeing but also feeling the light. Is this what being in love is really like? Why does it feel so fragile, like the crystal lake is glimmering but only until the dam breaks? When your rose-colored glasses eventually *smash, how can you ever return to* the *darkness again?*

Insecurity

I think I can't let go and trust
because I'm still waiting
for you to turn around and leave.

I keep waiting-
for you to see the ugliness
the others saw.
The one that made a boy   go from
I love you
to
I hate you
in what felt like   moments.

I'm waiting for you to
throw me away-
put the knife in my
back.
Give me more scars,
add to my
collection.

It's hard to feel
I'm worth loving.

*Can't you see what a fucking
mess I am?*

It's all I see.

Every scar you kiss lightens under your touch. Loving you feels like the deep breath you take right after an anxiety attack is over. The one where you realize the ground is still underneath you and you're still here. You have a way of reminding my heart and mind that they should be holding hands, not fighting a war.

A Poet Falling in   *Love*

I've been looking for the words
since I knew my ABCs,
but they've escaped every time.
Never fluid enough,
never the right phrase.

It wasn't
until you
spelled It out-
on my neck,
down my spine-
was I able to see
them
clearly.

The poetry is all over,
our unmade bed.
My words found me-
through you.

I thought sadness made a writer-
and maybe that's partially true.
But never did I understand the written word
as well as when you made me breakfast in bed.

Thank you for helping me find my words,
the universe brought you to me and now-
the dictionary will never be the same,
not since I found you.

There's something about loving you- I'm quite fond of it.
So much so- I think I'll do it the rest of my life.

Lessons In Love

My first love was a boy with bronze skin and green eyes. He woke up my little 16-year-old heart to what first love felt like. Feelings exploded out of me; nothing else was worth breathing for, a desperation that came from the girl who never felt good enough. I lost myself to the boy with golden hair. He made me love him so much I didn't love anything else, not even myself. When he realized he had love to give to many more girls, he broke my heart and let me let him go.

"Well, do you still love me?"
"I don't know."
"I guess that's my answer."

My second love was a hipster guy with a scratchy beard and a kind heart. He looked into my 18-year-old brown eyes and wanted to know what it meant to love. He showed me what being in love with your best friend could feel like, someone to love me for the girl I wanted to be. But being someone's first love again was a mistake; the boy with big dreams didn't know how to love. Choosing him was a choice I paid for. Twice.

"I just don't want a girlfriend anymore."
Was I so expendable to you? Am I even worth shedding a tear for?

My forever love, six-feet-tall and arms that feel like home. You came into the world of a 19-year-old when all she wanted was to break hearts and cry herself to sleep alone. My dream man, the one who looks at me as if I am whole when all I see are shattered pieces. A relationship built on love, trust, friendship, and commitment. My best of both worlds. All I want is to build a life with you, hand in hand.

"I'll love you forever and a day- but not a day longer."

I think you can love more than one person, but never quite the same way. My first love taught me passion, and my second love taught me companionship. Now, I can love my person effortlessly. I'm grateful for the lessons in love, and now I get to be loved the right way.

Finally.

Never look at my poetry as a cry for help.

Instead, look between these pages with smile and pride because I won. I manipulated those monsters hanging around every corner and trapped them here. These pages are my heaven and hell- they're my way of healing. If in them you find something special to touch your heart, I hope we can share in that together.

Please know you are always here; rest assured, the demons are locked away- stuck in the ink.

They'll never hurt us now.

About Kelsey Rojas:

Kelsey was born in hectic Brooklyn, New York but was raised in the quiet suburbs of Pennsylvania. After graduating from high school in 2012, she went to Philadelphia University to study Fashion Merchandising and Management. As she went on to continue her professional career in retail, the love for writing was always there, holding her hand and waiting for her to see herself.

As a young girl, Kelsey battled with finding a true passion. Her dreams ranged from marine biologist to Britney Spears, and she never quite knew who she was. In middle school, she moved and found herself bullied for the first time. Her reaction was to abandon her creative spirit and become a chameleon. Never expressing what made her happy or cultivating her own sense of self, she sought others to create an image, transforming her personality to suit whatever boy said, "You're pretty" and whatever girl said, "We're best friends now."

When she found herself on the other side of an emotionally manipulative relationship and a life-altering trauma, she was forced to confront what she was most afraid of: herself. She realized she had no idea who she genuinely was, but as she searched inward to understand herself, her poetry began to flow again. A way to heal her heart was slowly becoming her greatest passion. She saw herself as a time traveler, allowing her to touch parts of her brain and heart she'd repressed and shut down.

Kelsey decided to take control of her life and make her art a bigger part of it. She created her poetry page on Instagram in 2019 and has been featured in online magazines and poetry pages. She continues her day job working in online commerce for a major retailer, but by night she's her dream: a writer with nothing but a pen, paper, and a head full of flowers.

To connect with Kelsey:

Poetry Instagram: https://www.instagram.com/kels_andherwords/

Illustrator Instagram: https://www.instagram.com/creativanyc/

And So, She Goes On

Nicole Barker

January 28, 2015. 3:45 in the morning. It's snowing, slippery, and I am in a car having a full-on panic attack because I have a gut feeling that I'm about to go to jail. No one in their right mind would be out at this time except strung-out drug addicts. The driver and I stop to get gas. I say, "This is not a good idea, considering this is where all the cops gas up before their shifts." We leave, pull up to the stoplight, and of course, it's red. Just my luck. Right then, police lights turn on. I think to myself, *This isn't happening. I'm just paranoid.* I have been up for God knows how long on bath salts, the drug that eats away at your physical, mental, and spiritual well-being. I ask, *Why me?* I knew it was time. I wasn't "Nicole" in any sense anymore. I didn't want to keep killing myself, but I sure as hell didn't want to go to jail.

Two cops approach the car, one on his side and one on mine. They start shining their flashlights at the car windows. I keep telling myself, *You're not going to jail. They won't find what's in your bra.* They ask for our IDs and why we are out at this time of morning. Of course, the story he tells them is ridiculous. I figure the cops know we're either selling or going to get dope. They go back to their car to check our credentials. The whole time they're gone, I'm asking myself, *Why, Nicole? Why did you do this to your life again?* The last three years of my relapse is going through my head.

The cops are back and I hear, "Step out and put your hands up." Before I get both feet on the ground, I am thrown to the pavement with a foot on my back and guns pointed. I think to myself, *What the hell is happening?* I'm mad and enraged, but I know this could go south really quick, so I stay silent. The cops start asking questions, interrogating me right then and there. I wasn't wanted, but I was involved with some dark individuals. The cops still assumed I was a suspect in this tragedy even though I was cleared weeks before.

Within minutes, a female officer arrives. I spread my legs and raise my arms. She says, "I can see you're layered." I say, "Yes, it's the middle of winter." She tells me to unlayer, and right then, I know I'm going to jail. She reads me my rights while I zone out. In a way, I'm relieved. I knew I couldn't stop the bath salts. No other drug in my entire life had me by my soul the way this one did.

We pull into the sally port at the police station, where people who have been arrested are unloaded and booked. As soon as processing is done, I am thrown into a cell. When I hear the loud slam of the metal door, I know this is the end; there is no coming back from this. I sit there in earth-shattering shock and just want to die. I am so ashamed and consumed with hate for myself. Only 33 years old and I had thrown everything away again: my life, my kids, and anyone who stepped into my path. Incarceration was nothing new to me, but I wasn't 18 anymore. This time, it was gut-wrenching. I stare at the grey walls and the women sleeping. My thoughts are like a sick, cyclical carousel. I can't escape them.

Hours turn into days. I don't call anyone to let them know where I am. I don't deserve comfort or to be told it was going to be okay, because it wasn't going to be okay. The chaos and wreckage I had caused so many could never be forgiven. There is no way to numb the emotions that are drowning within me, but I deserve to feel every bit of the anguish. Days turn into weeks, then months.

One morning after headcount, I pick up the phone to call my mother. To my surprise, she answers. I really have nothing to say except, "Yep, I destroyed everything again." I am shocked to learn that my mom had been following my case. All she keeps saying is, "I'm begging you, please take drug court." Drug court is an intense, 24-month outpatient treatment with many strict rules and guidelines; most do not make it all the way through. I tell her, "No way, not happening." I wasn't about to have my entire life under a damn microscope. I had already made up my mind that I would do the prison time. Besides, drug court wouldn't bring my kids back to me. It wouldn't bring back my sister, who I took care of on and off throughout the years and destroyed with my actions. She depended on me for love, support, nurturing, and sisterhood. My sister looked up to me and we were very close until I completely destroyed her trust in me. If that wasn't enough, I also said the most painful, disgusting things that one person could say to another. No one deserves to be spoken to the way I did her that day. I wasn't sure if I could ever look at myself again; I'd always be thinking about the way I caused her so much trauma and brokenness. Too much damage had been done. Why in God's name would I set myself up for failure by taking drug court? Plus, I deserve to be locked up for all the wreckage I had caused the ones who meant more to me than life itself.

Lindsey, my bunkmate in my cell, asks me, "Do you want better?" She says, "You deserve better. Don't give up on yourself, your daughters, or your sister." A few more weeks go by, and I keep contemplating everything Lindsey said to me. I know for sure that I hated drugs and that I never want to hurt my girls or sisters ever again. Even if they could never forgive me, I owe it to myself, my daughters, and my sisters to fight for my life. I want to give them their mom and sister back.

Satan came into my head, saying, "You're worthless, you will never get them back." Realistically, what future did I have ahead? This is my third felony. I've never had a real job, and it was nearly impossible to find a home. Felonies make it almost unfeasible to have any life, and that's what Satan keeps telling me.

It's now two weeks until my sentencing. My public defender tells me that the prosecution will charge me with "habitual offender," meaning I could face 15 or more years in prison unless I take drug court. In all honesty, I'm not willing to risk that much prison time. As the days get closer, a fire is burning within me. Something clicks that God has big plans for me. I don't know how to explain it, and even though it seems completely impossible to do drug court, I am being pushed by something to take it. Today, I realize it was the Holy Spirit, but I didn't know it then. I want better; my girls and my sisters deserve better from me. I'm willing to do whatever it takes, including accepting that people I destroyed may not be able to get past the wreckage I caused them.

In May 2015, I enter the Ada County Drug Court program in Boise, Idaho. I am court-ordered to live in the women's homeless shelter, where I reside for almost eight months. Another requirement of my treatment program is absolutely zero contact with my mom and brother. They are triggers, and we had used together in the past. I keep thinking, *How in the world am I gonna do this all alone? But, I got high on my own.*

It's lonely in the shelter. My family has the opportunity to be in my life as long as they submit to random urine tests. Needless to say, it doesn't happen. Before, my recovery was on my terms and I truly thought I knew how to stay sober. I know that this time, I had to submit. I had to accept a new way of life and a new way to continue to be clean. If I truly and authentically wanted that, I had to dig deep, do each and every step of work.

Drug court keeps you busy. It's like having a full-time job and a part-time job, and I'm exhausted. The program is 24 months with four phases. I feel hopelessness, sadness, and loneliness. Satan is putting in extra work on me. I want to share this new me and this new life with my family. My children all live in different states, and my sisters have no idea where they are. I'm hurt that my family decided not to step up and be part of my new life. Am I not important enough? Today, I know it was addiction still leading their lives. I knew it then as well, but I assumed that the opportunity to see me would be their motivation. It hurts me to the core and makes me doubt my future after graduating drug court. Who would I really have? Would my kids and sisters be able to forgive me? I keep pushing and fighting, regardless of the lies going through my head.

Here I am, moving up to phase three. Wow, what an amazing accomplishment! I love the woman I see in the mirror. I see her magic resurfacing. Within a few weeks, I am asked to relay a message from my brother to a guy named Scott, so I look him up on Facebook. From there, I find the love of my life.

The story of how my husband and I came about is incredible and truly magical. It sounds so cliché, right? It almost seems too good to be true. When I met my future husband, I realized he was also struggling with addiction. It was pretty risky to be interested in him, but something felt different about him and this situation. He told me that my strength, success, and devotion to my recovery made him want better for his life, too. My future husband wanted better for himself and truly wanted to be a part of my life.

He told me he was signing up for random urine tests. I couldn't believe it. No one in my whole entire life other than my daddy had ever invested in me the way Scott did. I had only known him for a little over four months, and he was willing to do this for me. It didn't seem real. I thought, *Is this really happening?* This man did something for me that my own family members wouldn't do. I've never had anyone do something for me without a motive. In this season of my life, I exploded with gratitude, hope, and so much more. I had changed someone's life with all the hard work, dedication, and devotion I had put into myself. Deep within, my magic had helped another human find himself and his recovery.

Graduation day is here! I see my now husband and stepchildren in the audience watching me accomplish something that seemed so impossible, and it is the absolute best feeling in the entire world. I chose to live and fight those demons. In return, I had a whole new life.

Remember the job, home, and life I believed to be impossible to obtain? I never believed I could find true peace and happiness, but today, it's all mine. Don't get me wrong, my family and I have struggled and felt hopeless throughout the years. However, it's over real-life situations like finances, loss, and pandemics, not drugs. With every storm, there's a rainbow. Even though things don't always turn out how we want them to, we're still alive, sober, and fighting for a better way of life.

When I decided to surrender and submit to a new way of life, I received more than I could have ever dreamed of. My testimony is my magic, and I will spend the rest of my life sharing it. I will also continue to help others to find theirs. Never, ever give in or give up. I believe with every ounce of my soul that if you truly want a better way of life, you can have it. Nothing is impossible. Your magic will shine again. I went through the trenches of darkness and despair. I fell many times, sometimes even crawling, but continued to keep my eyes forward and my mind surrounded with the magic glowing inside of me. I allowed myself to feel the pain and ripped through each obstacle. Through my pain and trials, I am the woman I am today.

One thing I remind myself of often is that I am not my past and everything has happened *to* me. I am everything I became through the healing, and I am no longer broken. I am so thankful for everything I have been through because it's made me the woman I am today. Today, I have an amazing life. I want to thank my husband for growing and investing in the woman I became. By the grace of God and His impeccable timing, I have restored the most precious relationships in my life.

I will be an addict until the day I die, but I don't have to die an active addict. Addiction is a lonely, dark place, but recovery doesn't have to be. I am so thankful I found the road to recovery and a new way of life. Believe in yourself. Let the magic flow through and out of you. Trust the process and surround yourself with authentic humans who are on the same road you are on.

As I sit and write this, I still can't believe this is happening. If someone told me six years ago while sitting on that bunk in jail that I would be engaged in such a precious project, I never would have believed them. Over the past few years, the desire to reach out and help others find a new way of life and find their own magic has been weighing heavily on my heart. I know that in time, that dream will fall into existence in my life. I am strong, worthy, loved, wanted, beautiful, and blessed. And so, she goes on!

About Nicole Barker:

Nicole is 39 years old and was born in Miami, Florida. She was raised by her grandparents Bill and Faye in Hillsborough, North Carolina. At the age of 12, she moved to Boise, Idaho with her mother and went on to live with her father in Grants, New Mexico. For the last 15 years, she has resided in Boise and Meridian, Idaho.

Nicole is married to her biggest fan and best friend, Scott. They have six extraordinary children from the ages of 11 to 23, five grandchildren, and of course, two fur babies Sissy and King. Nicole is a full-time finish carpenter for a modular building company. She has worked for the company since early 2017 and she has a lot of pride in her job. Nicole's job gives her the opportunity to learn new skills and is something she enjoys.

When Nicole isn't working, she invests her time in her family. Being the mama of six children keeps you on your toes! She is forever grateful and appreciative for the time she gets to invest in her children. Nicole's recovery and walk with the Lord are at the top of her priority list, along with self-care and self-love. She absolutely loves crafting, decorating, and the great outdoors of Idaho.

Nicole has goals for her future, such as digging deeper in her faith with the Lord so she can someday be able to minister to those who are searching for Him. She also intends to go back to school to earn a certificate to help others struggling with addiction, domestic violence, and depression. It would be her dream to help and work with children and teens. Lastly, Nicole will someday write a solo book of her own.

Nicole would like to let anyone reading this chapter know that she believes in you, that anything is possible, and that she can be contacted below.

To connect with Nicole:

Facebook: https://www.facebook.com/profile.php?id=100014692234389

Email: nicolebarker429@gmail.com

Instagram: https://www.instagram.com/scottnicolebarker/

TikTok: https://vm.tiktok.com/ZMeDp15Fe/

Free To Be Me

Susan Finkel Barrows

This is a story about finding clarity around your life's purpose and vision after a series of radical steps, including divorce, that lead to a spiritual awakening. It is about having the courage to find your voice in the face of adversity and accepting that there are many ways to grow and find your authentic self.

December 3, 2017 was the day I went from a marriage that I hoped we could salvage to being shockingly single. It also happened to be our 12th anniversary. As we were heading to our favorite restaurant for dinner, I started talking about an article that I had just read in the *New York Times*. It made an impression on me because it was about a couple navigating divorce and new relationships while always putting their kids first, no matter what. I thought this was so powerful and healthy that two people could remain amicable for their children. I mentioned this idea to my partner Karina. I said that if we ever considered getting a divorce, we always would put our kids first. We would try to remain amicable friends for the children to reduce any psychological effect this change in our relationship might have on them. After all, we chose to bring these kids into this world, and we owed it to ourselves to try to raise healthy children into adulthood. Divorce can be difficult, but if we could find it possible to be supportive of each other in the midst of our children's watchful eyes, it would hopefully help them as they adjusted to their new normal.

Talking about this article was a foreshadowing of our new lives and a catalyst for Karina to finally bring up how she truly felt. It takes such courage to know when it is time to end a marriage, and we both intrinsically knew that the relationship was over. We were not happy. However, I never imagined in a million years that we would give up on ourselves on this night or that she would be the first to ask for a separation.

After the shock, anger, and sadness wore off from this conversation, my life changed drastically. This devastating and traumatic period has since taught me more about love and courage than I ever thought possible. Parts of me that had laid dormant for so long were able to come to the surface. For me, it ended up being an optimistic act, a belief that there might be a happier future waiting for me if I could survive the adjustments of going it alone. The pieces of me that I never even knew about started unraveling as I was given a chance to figure out who I was. Take my hand as I tell you a bit about my spiritual awakening that changed my life in so many amazing and transformative ways.

The first step in my transformational journey was to find a mindful therapist. This simple act started to pave the way for me to start on my inner healing. I wanted to heal and love *me* so I would be whole as a person and a mother. We did a lot of different types of meditation, visualization, and journaling. We focused on increasing my awareness around my feelings and actions in trying to cultivate more positive emotions and outlook in life. What I learned during my six months gave me the breadcrumbs to seek out other teachers and books with a thirst for metamorphosis.

Next on my journey, I found healing through reiki. Through several reiki sessions, which use a form of energy to heal, I had a profound healing experience. It led me to want to become a reiki healer. I became attuned to reiki one and two by a dear friend and became a Usui Reiki Master and Teacher a year later. A beautiful aspect of reiki is that the energy is always available, and the healing energy always knows where to heal.

One of the things that surfaced during my reiki sessions was this feeling that I never had a voice. I had always prided myself on being flexible, going with the flow, and being very agreeable. However, I never realized that in actuality, these practices were giving up pieces of myself. I was like a chameleon, becoming what I needed to be as a mother, wife, or daughter to keep everyone else happy. By recognizing that I needed to speak my truth, I began to learn how to heal more inner trauma. I began to understand that by consistently backing down and not speaking my truth, I was muting who I was and losing my sense of self. These practices resulted in killing my spirit. Martin Luther King, Jr. said, "There comes a time when silence is betrayal," and I was betraying myself by being silent. I needed to take my voice back.

As I was healing myself, I was turning more towards love and away from fear. As I turned from negativity, I found that many doors opened. I was shown positive messages from various teachers to further my spiritual learning. After opening the spiritual door with my reiki journey, I fell down the proverbial rabbit hole. I began to watch video after video on intriguing topics like quantum physics and the Law of Attraction on YouTube from people like Esther Hicks, Jack Canfield, Marianne Williamson, Michael B. Beckwith, Louise Hay, and finally, Gabrielle Bernstein. I was looking for a spiritual guru, someone with whom I truly resonated, to guide me to the next level in my transformation.

After listening to so many people, I kept coming back to Gabrielle. Like me, she was Jewish, and I listened to her talk over and over about her transformation. She was so warm, believable, and espoused many of the same ideas as all the other individuals that I had listened to. She opened up this whole new world of self-love, forgiveness, and a holistic approach to spirituality for me. Through her books, videos, and meditations, I found a deeper connection to a higher power. This helped further facilitate my healing and reduce my limiting beliefs.

In reading Gabrielle's books *The Universe Has Your Back: Transform Fear to Faith* and *Super Attractor: Methods for Manifesting a Life Beyond Your Wildest Dreams*, I found I had a toolkit with steps on how to live my life with a clearer purpose. I started to understand how beliefs and feelings can truly change one's whole outlook on life, from limiting beliefs to receiving abundance. I learned about turning my guidance over to a higher power. In this surrender, I began to shift my focus from fear and anxiety. I learned how to continually get back in alignment with the energy of peace, love, and joy. During this shift, I was able to remove many of my limiting beliefs and blocks as I learned that the universe was always there to support me. One of the largest mindset transformations was cultivating an appreciation for what I had and creating an attitude of gratitude that I could turn to daily. As I changed, I felt such a sense of joy and serenity show up in my life; I was attracting what I needed.

After seeing Gabby speak in San Francisco in support of her latest book, I was very excited to take things to the next level. As I sat in the audience surrounded by this amazing feminine energy, an idea took shape in my mind: I should think about helping other women heal through positive transformations as I had. One of the signs from the universe that I was on the right path came when I was explaining my dreams to a colleague. I wanted to heal others with reiki, sound healing, and work collaboratively with others from my spiritual community on beautiful weekend retreats. We were outside under this immense sweet acacia tree when I started explaining my passionate dreams out loud for the first time. All of a sudden, all the birds in the tree started chirping *loudly*. It went from silence to a deafening cacophony, then died down to normal sounds. After hearing this, we both turned to each other and said this *had* to be a sign! We talked about this for weeks. Every time I remembered that sign from the universe, I knew my path was starting to be revealed to me. This surreal experience truly showed me that I was being guided by a higher power. This was not a coincidence nor a random event; this was a deep, symbolic event. The universe was telling me that I was finally understanding my path in life.

I was starting to understand my evolution. I was not here as a passive bystander or spectator anymore, and I was being given a vision into my gifts and talents. With growing understanding, I realized that doors were opening and showing me limitless possibilities. I was focusing more on unconditional love, compassion, joy, and peace as qualities that embodied who I was becoming. I believe that these changes led me to Michelle Eades' amazing tribe of like-minded people on Facebook called the "Joyful Warriors." Individuals in this community became a lifeline for me when the pandemic hit in March 2020. Michelle provided us with a magical community in which we found connections that made us feel less alone. She guided us in how to work with oracle cards as well as exploring our past lives, something that Michelle is known for. Through this group, I met some amazing individuals virtually and discovered that a few of us were even connected in many previous lifetimes.

As isolation continued due to COVID-19 throughout 2020 and into 2021, my daily routine of meditation, journaling, and visualization both grounded me and allowed me to transform. Despite such troubling times, I was able to come out of my shell and become one of the most positive people I knew. Day after day, I was able to keep myself positive when so many others were struggling. A light bulb went off, and I felt like my new goal in life was to support others; it was like an epiphany. With guidance on visualizing a better life, I wanted to teach people how positivity, positive affirmations, and meditation could provide a positive, evolutionary shift in awareness.

I created a Facebook group called "The Guiding Light" to become a place like "Joyful Warriors" had been for me. It became a safe place where people could share the magic of positivity, meditation, journaling, vision boards, and life visioning to find positive solutions and desired outcomes. I wanted to be like a guiding light to struggling people while providing the support and positive energy of unconditional divine love as guidance for changing lives. As my messages connected within the community, people started reaching out to me to let me know that my words were making an important and positive impact. The idea that my encouraging energy was making a positive impression filled me with vast feelings of love, gratefulness, and appreciation. New, beautiful doors started to open for me, like a kaleidoscope of possibilities to live my life to its highest potential.

Here are a few items in my magical toolkit that I have used to develop a more positive mindset, especially in the last year:

1. Keep a gratitude journal where you keep track of three to five things each day that you are grateful for.
2. Create simple, empowering, positive affirmations that help create something new in your life. For example, I have one that I carry with me everywhere: I am so happy and grateful that love and abundance flow into my life!
3. Create a habit of meditating every day. Meditation and deep breathing, even for only five minutes, can help you reach a calm and relaxed state.
4. Do something joyful and creative, like sending Happy Mail to friends. Happy Mail is mail that makes people happy, like sending a smile through the mail.
5. Surround yourself with positive people who are like sunshine and make you laugh, inspire you, and lift your spirits.

I have been able to completely change my mindset since I started from that place of anger, anxiety, and the scary unknowns of becoming a successful single mother. I now know that the universe does indeed have my back. I have come to believe that a good outcome can come from believing in yourself and that you can manifest your success by putting your trust in a higher power. Out of the ashes of divorce, I have been reborn. I have discovered insights into my true purpose: to help and guide others as an energy healer and a Positive Mindset Coach, and an amazing mother. In adopting a more positive mindset and a want to help others through struggles similar to mine, I have come to realize that I have become much more resilient and adept at coping with stressful situations. All it takes is reframing your thoughts from something negative to something more positive, replacing limiting beliefs, and rewriting your story with a fresh, new narrative filled with promise. If I could re-write my narrative, be open to creative and new possibilities, and find success after divorce, so can you! Always remember to inhale *confidence*, exhale *fear*, and know that you are always perfect just the way you are.

About Susan Finkel Barrows:

Susan is an energy healer, positive mindset influencer, and writer. She has been on a spiritual journey for at least the last three years, which has been a guiding light in her life. During the COVID-19 pandemic in 2020, she was called to create positive and uplifting messages that combined her love of positive affirmations and graphic design. She began to spread the power of positivity across social media and in return, brightened people's lives like sprinkles of pixie dust.

Susan was born and raised in Lansdale, Pennsylvania. After graduating high school from North Penn in 1987, she attended and graduated from Ursinus College in Collegeville, Pennsylvania. While studying German, Spanish, and French in college, she traveled during the summers, sparking her love of travel and international cultures. Susan is an avid lover of meditation, reiki, photography, and all things tech. She currently lives in Phoenix, Arizona and is a mom to three amazing children: Greyson, Georgia, Gianna, and one chocolate dachshund named Sassy.

To connect with Susan:

Facebook: https://www.facebook.com/susan.finkel/

Instagram: https://www.instagram.com/thesiouxsieque/

LinkedIn: https://www.linkedin.com/in/susanfinkel/

Believe in the Magic of You

Traci Miller

As I walked down the hall with my back to him, trying to keep my shoulders from slumping forward as the tears made their way down my cheeks, I wondered if that was the last time I'd see him alive. What if it was? What then?

Dan and I had celebrated our 23rd wedding anniversary the previous October. It was such an unmemorable experience; I honestly have no idea if we even said the words "Happy Anniversary" to each other. There's a lot you take for granted when you're married for that long. It's not intentional, of course. Nonetheless, it happens, and it had happened to us. The magic had been replaced with complacency. However, I didn't realize the extent of the damage until almost a year later.

We'd raised five kids mostly into adulthood. We'd also raised Dan's manufacturing company from the ground up in the same time period. Yet, as I sat in the waiting room of the hospital, I felt personally devalued. How had I let my dreams of accomplishing great things in the world get smaller as my kids got bigger? We had planned for me to be a stay-at-home mom, but for some unknown reason, we had never planned for when or if I would go back to work.

So, here I was: waiting to hear whether or not I was going to be a widow at the age of 47 with no job and no way to support my family because I had become complacent about my dreams as I helped my husband build his. How the hell did I not go back to work when all the kids were in school full-time? How did I not value myself enough to stand up for the dreams I once had? How did I not see that I was teaching my daughters to put everyone else ahead of themselves?

As I sat there playing out the worst-case scenario for my husband in my mind, I also dared to dream of the best scenario for me. Ironically, in that hour when I didn't know if I still had a husband, my dreams didn't seem frivolous, meaningless, or selfish. They were the magical hope that I clung to. Even if the worst happened, I knew what I could, should, and wanted to do, regardless of the news the doctor was coming to tell me.

Friday, March 10, 2017 was the day it all changed. It was the day I *decided* change, or so I thought. It seemed like a simple decision, but it turned out to be a not-so easy journey. That day, my husband lived. He fought to live and I started to fight for the dreams I decided I wanted to achieve. As we all know, deciding to do something and actually implementing it do not always align. With the imminent emergency no longer staring me in the face, I slipped back into my old, comfy life. It was different in some respects, but still had the same familiar comfort of taking care of everyone else, making sure everyone else had what they needed, and consuming information on how I could, someday, maybe, build a magical online business.

I'd always been an entrepreneur, even before the term was mainstream. I had a paper route. I'd been a babysitter. I was the neighborhood "boy" pushing the lawnmower and snowblower down the sidewalk, stopping at the houses where I knew the elderly folks lived. I have been called "sonny" more times than I care to remember.

After my oldest daughter was born, I started a landscape design company called Hoeing Around. Yep, catchy but not professional nor profitable with a baby in tow. So, I pivoted to making candles with my husband and created matching scented mulch for houseplants. I carted the candles and mulch to craft shows all over northeast Ohio. With a couple more babies hanging on my legs, prioritizing myself and the business I was trying to build slowly slipped away. The internet had just become a thing, and work from home opportunities were anything but the norm.

Once we reached full capacity with five kids, we moved to a bigger house in a great school district. Surrounded by white collar geniuses in a town where you could run into entrepreneurs like the founder of Little Tykes at the grocery store, my husband started a manufacturing company and started to build his legacy. The kids and I helped, but it had always been his dream and his business. I was happy to support him, until one day a couple months after Dan's heart attack, I realized just how "his" everyone believed the business was. That day, my 15-year-old son, innocently although no less painfully, said to me that he needed some of "dad's money" to go shopping.

I felt invisible. Completely invisible, completely unappreciated, and it really pissed me the eff off. How dare they? After everything I sacrificed for them, how dare they believe that it was "dad's money" because he went to work and I didn't? Before he started his business, Dan and I had a conversation about how hard it was going to be to grow the manufacturing company and raise our family. He knew he couldn't do it without me taking all of the responsibility of the house and the kids. He told me my job was to help him not worry about anything at home. But, the kids didn't know that we'd had that conversation. So, here I sat: completely dumbfounded, thoroughly angry, and extremely disappointed again, mostly in myself, for having given up on the magic of my dreams.

That night, I told Dan that I wanted to build an online business. I told him about the all-consuming information I had been researching on how to create, market, and sell online courses to help women build Etsy stores. Had Etsy been around with our candle and mulch business, I explained, I probably wouldn't have stopped doing it. Now, these women, these moms, had opportunities I didn't, and I could use my experience to help them. After all, I was a high school teacher before we had kids. I'd always had a natural love for teaching people, starting back in the fourth grade when I was a math tutor during lunch recess. What I didn't know how to do so well was create videos for marketing and teaching purposes, but I had found an online coach to help me that I wanted to invest in.

The conversation that ensued was nothing short of a punch that I never saw coming. The man who had pointedly told me I brought as much value to our family by doing what I did at home, even though it wasn't directly attached to making money as he did building his manufacturing company for our legacy, told me that if I wanted to invest in a coach to help me with video marketing, I needed to get clients first to pay for the coach. He told me that he believed that online coaches were a scam, I could Google everything I needed to learn, and that he wasn't giving me money to invest in someone like that.

Giving me money.

Those were the words that hurt the most, and the ones I did not expect him to say. It felt as though my entire identity as an equal adult in our house was a lie. I couldn't let myself succumb to the thoughts that I was "just" a mom, so I decided to get a job to earn the money I needed to hire the coach. Those words would become the very definition of how others saw me.

As I turned over the application to the human resources person, he asked if I had an additional sheet with my employment history on it. I said I hadn't had any W-2 jobs since before my daughter was born, and the application had only asked for the last five years of employment history. Of course, my history was older than that. He said, "Oh, so you're just a mom looking for a job as something to do while the kids are in school, then?" My heart broke.

As I walked out to the car, the tears came, the same as they did that day in the hospital when Dan had his heart attack. I tried to walk with my shoulders pulled back. I tried not to let the tears fall. Once I reached the car, I put my arms on the steering wheel, buried my head in my arms, and sobbed. I sobbed for who I had become, for who I wasn't, and for who I thought I would be. Then, I screamed while hitting the steering wheel. I'm sure I looked like a crazy person, and I felt like one. I just needed someone, anyone, to believe in me half as much as I believed in me. Just one. Just one "someone".

Then, I realized who it was. Who it always had been, and who it *needed* to be.

The only person who could believe in me was *me*.

The only person who it needed to be was *me*.

In order for anyone to believe in *me*, I had to believe in *me* first.

I had to believe in me for everyone who didn't, even if they were my husband, my kids, or my friends. Unless and until I was willing to stand in my own power, stand up for my own damn self, and stand out as the woman I was created to be, no one else would or could ever do it for me. That realization, that reckoning, was the real starting point of my magical journey. Yes, I had decided to change and go after my dreams the day my husband had his heart attack, but it wasn't until I decided that I had to do it for myself, not because my kids needed me to do it, that the real magic of my journey started to appear.

Since that day, the universe has had my back.

She has brought the teachers and coaches I needed into my life at exactly the moment I needed them.

She has given me the courage to stand alone so that I could help others not have to stand alone.

She has helped me up when I've fallen and has shown me the magic in learning how to avoid the same fall again.

She has shown me the magic in getting results for the sake of getting results and how not to put judgment on them.

She has raised my dreams from a baby to a teenager on the cusp of creating a global impact.

She has surrounded me in magic through the goodness of strangers to help me on my journey.

She has shown me the magic in my own heart and that, if you're willing to surrender to it, there's just as much magic in helping yourself as there is in helping others.

She has shown me that She works in mysterious ways, and that even a left-brained logical person like me can't avoid the signs of magic, even if I can't wrap it in a logic bow.

She has put her magical stamp on my Pink PowerHouse brand when others didn't believe in naming it that and even though I don't like the color pink, which is a whole other magical story for another book.

Mostly, She has shown me that the magic I thought I lost, the magic I thought I gave up on, the magic that I didn't know I still had in me, was waiting on *me* to decide that I was ready, willing, and determined to bring it to life, for *me*. She has shown me that only through recognizing my own magic am I able to see the magic in others and give magic to others.

So, if you want magic, if you're waiting on magic, if you're looking for magic…then you need to decide to first believe in the magic of you.

About Traci Miller:

Traci Miller, born, raised, and living in the suburbs of Cleveland, Ohio is an unapologetic success strategist, mindset mentor, and CEO of The Pink PowerHouse Co. She's on a mission to elevate the worth and wealth of women for generations because no woman should ever have to choose between family and financial freedom. Traci's specialty is helping high-achieving yet cash poor multi-six and seven-figure powerhouse women to master the deeper self-worth issues behind their unwillingness to raise their prices, break through the unseen money story that's holding them back, and position themselves worthy of up-leveling into their next figure of profits.

Traci combines her background as an ambitious entrepreneur, having created her first company when she was 12, with a deep mastery of coaching focused on bespoke solutions and a love of mathematical analytics (complete with math trophies) to help women make strategic mediocre to million dollar changes that ultimately change their life and their legacy.

Her biggest accomplishment by far is raising her five beautiful children with her husband of 28 years. A close second is overcoming 17 years of depression as a stay-at-home mom where she lost her self, but found her worth.

To connect with Traci:

Facebook: https://www.facebook.com/groups/pinkpowerhousesociety/

Instagram: www.instagram.com/iamtracimiller

Clubhouse: https://www.joinclubhouse.com/club/pinkpowerhousesociety

My Journey to a 5D Marriage

Stephanie Mahony

We've all been there, ladies: hiding under our sheets, crying over another failed relationship, trying to figure out what happened, and being terrified to start over again. No matter where we live or what language we speak, love is a universal truth that we all understand. The problem is, many of us get stuck feeling like things will never change. That was my story, anyway. For years, I was so unlucky in love while my friends were flourishing in happy relationships. I couldn't catch a break, never felt good enough, and kept attracting the wrong guys. I became the girl that everyone felt sorry for. But thankfully, my story doesn't end there. Today, I want to share my journey with you: how I overcame hardships, transformed my mindset, and manifested my soulmate.

When Love Don't Come Easy

"Nothing ever goes away until it teaches us what we need to know." - Pema Chodron

Growing up, I was one of those girls who had it all figured out. I had mapped out my future from a young age, and by 25, I was going to be married with kids. Unfortunately, fate didn't unfold that way. At 26 years old I was still single, miserable, and nowhere close to my plan. For years, I had been in a controlling and narcissistic relationship where I lost my identity, my friends, and my self-worth. It broke me to my core. I felt like I had wasted years after the relationship ended trying to find myself again, to rebuild my friendships and my confidence, and to trust in people. Eventually, I was able to push forward and I met a person I was falling for. In my heart, I knew he wasn't meant for my future, so I cut the cord and walked away, secretly crying. I slowly started dating again. I even attempted blind dates, but got stood up by two separate guys. *Why am I not good enough?*

Then, I found him. My dream guy, and the one I eventually end up calling "The Bay Street Asshole." His charismatic personality wooed me over, but I quickly learned that I was second in life to his friends, his job, and his interests. He literally had no desire to know me as a person. I was more like a trophy wife that he only displayed when it was convenient. But, I thought he was "the one," so I tried my best to fight for the relationship. I made myself look perfect, act perfectly, say the things he wanted to hear, and brush it away when he treated me badly. *Give him another chance. This HAS to work.* Nothing ever impressed him. I found myself in the same cycle of losing myself. This time, I had become fake, unauthentic, and shallow. I was so caught up in trying to be perfect that I became crippled with the anxiety of not being good enough. For the first time ever, I was prescribed pills to help ease me through it. Months and months later, I finally walked away. My dream was crushed, and was I devasted to have to start over again.

Eventually, I did meet another charming guy. A little nerdy, super cute, and someone I would not normally date. However, he was always so distant. Six months later, I found out he was dating someone else at the same time. My heart was completely shattered. I had never felt so deceived and I hit rock bottom. I knew I was being tested and couldn't understand why I kept failing. I was mad at myself, mad at these experiences, and mad at God. I thought to myself, *I go to church, I read the Bible, and I'm a good person. Why can't I catch a break?!* By this time, my friends were starting to get engaged. I was so happy for them, but cried to one of my girlfriends that I'd be that lonely cat lady when I grew up. I was so done with guys. I was so done with everyone.

This deep resentment seemed to attract more circumstances of feeling angry, upset, and like I was a victim. I hit new lows. Down in this lonely pit, I would dwell and feel sorry for myself; it was there where I hit yet another new low, which spun me into hopeless despair. However, something different happened this time. Instead of running away again, I turned around to face it. I dug my feet into the ground and energetically transmuted my anger: *Alright. Bring it on. No matter what you throw my way, I am going to be bigger than this. I will continue to be good to people, no matter what. I am going to find true love, no matter what. When I finally find it, I'm just gonna know. It will be love at first sight and we'll start our future quickly.* It came out so strongly, so boldly, and I meant every word of it. It felt more like an affirmation than a prayer. While those words kept circling around in my mind, I felt a tiny release, a tiny change in energy. It felt like I was in control again. I rolled up all the garbage in my spirit and offered it up to the universe. I surrendered it to God, telling Him this was in His hands now: *I have no idea what I'm doing, so I'm giving this all to you.*

An Energy Shift

*"A dream is a wish your heart makes, when you're fast asleep...
No matter how your heart is grieving, if you keep on believing, the dream
that you wish will come true."* -Mack David & Jerry Livingston, *Cinderella*

Soon after that incident, I was exhausted and just sought peace and solitude. I turned off music, TV, my phone, and would sit in stillness trying to reflect on life. As I laid there with my eyes closed, I started to see images play out in my mind like a movie strip. It was of this tall, handsome guy. He was blondish with these big arms. He would bend down, pick up two small kids, and swirl them around in circles. The sun behind them was shining so brightly that I couldn't see their faces. As I watched this play out over and over again, I knew in my heart this was real. It was like a glimpse into my future. My thoughts were filled with happiness: *That's him, the guy I've been searching for, and there he is playing with our kids. Oh my gosh!* The feeling was so warm, so real, and so comforting. I never wanted it to end. Even though it seemed like a lifetime away, I knew that somewhere, somehow, I was drawing him in. I could just feel it.

From that day on, I felt this sense of joy vibe throughout my day, and I began walking with this little pep in my step. I felt like my eyes were opening up to the world around me and I was becoming aware of things I never paid attention to before. I noticed the guy who dropped off his girlfriend in front of the restaurant so she wouldn't get wet from the rain. I admired the old couple eating ice cream together on a park bench. As I was doing household chores, I noticed the framed photo of my mom that my dad kept on his side of the bathroom counter, and the sticky notes they would leave each other around the house. It made my heart so happy. I thought, *One day, I'm going to have this, too.* I started listening to sappy love songs on repeat and began meditating on the words. My favorite was the 80s song, "Dream Come True" by Frozen Ghost. I sang along to these words pretending it was me, finally finding him. I thought to myself, *This is how I'm going to feel.*

My energy was lifting. I was feeling happier, lighter, and looking at life with a grateful heart. At night, I began reflecting on my past relationships. I began to see each of us as little children, like young souls, trying to figure it all out. I saw us just learning, growing, and trying our best to find love inside this great big world. By seeing our innocence, it made it easier for me to forgive each person, each situation, and even myself. I looked at each broken relationship as a lesson and took accountability for my part in things going wrong. I could understand it was teaching me what I truly wanted in a partner and how *I* could do better myself, too. As I looked down upon each of us young children, I prayed we'd each find the love we've been searching for. Somehow, this pure intention triggered a release. Suddenly, I could feel my body relax and that hard shell around my heart started to melt away. I just laid there in still calmness. Forgiveness was healing my soul. I went through the fire, but no longer smelled like smoke.

And So, It Begins

> *"You know you're in love when you can't fall asleep,*
> *because reality is finally better than your dreams."* -Dr. Seuss

My girlfriend met her husband online and was convinced I needed to get on there, too. She was tired of my cat stories and put together a profile for me. The thought of going online was terrifying: *What if someone I knew found me on there? What would they think?* However, secretly, I was grateful because I'd never go on myself. I spent lots of time searching profiles and met a bunch of nice people, but the summer was coming up, and I just wanted to enjoy it with my girlfriends.

One evening, I was trying to figure out how to delete my profile when suddenly, this gorgeous guy popped up. His name was Tim. He had this huge smile, beautiful eyes, and looked like this cozy teddy bear. His profile was so genuine, and even had a photo of him wearing a Mighty Mouse Halloween costume. I thought, *The guys on here post shirtless muscle photos of themselves, but this guy is adorable!* I was so drawn to his confidence and lightheartedness. I knew I had to message him, so I did, and we totally hit it off. A couple days later, he drove by my office so we could meet. He was even more gorgeous in real life and *so* funny.

A couple days after that, we went on our first date to a driving range, and there he was, helping me with my swing. As I nestled in between his arms, it triggered a memory: *I've imagined these big arms before.* We went for dinner shortly after, and when we walked inside the restaurant, he took off his sunglasses. It was the first time I saw him in person without them. I looked into his eyes and they immediately pierced me. I felt so dizzy walking to our table. My heart was racing and the menu looked blurry. I thought, *Oh my gosh, it's him. This is* him! It was in that moment that I really knew.

We chatted all night, but I don't remember a thing. I was a big ol' ball of nerves: excited, dizzy, nauseous, and already in love. I kept excusing myself to the bathroom and would poke out to make sure he was actually real. I kept thinking to myself, *After all these years of searching and searching, there he is sitting at table 214. I finally found him! He's even more perfect in real life.* After dinner, he walked me to the car. I was ready for him to make a move, but he gave me a kiss on the cheek, a hug, and walked away with a grin. I thought, *Oh my gosh, he's a gentleman, too.* I jumped into my car so jittery and picked up the phone to call my mother. I told her, "Mom, I met the guy I'm going to marry."

As fate would have it, everything fell into place so naturally. Nothing was a struggle and our lives fit perfectly together. Riding home from a cottage weekend is one of my earliest memories of me seeing how true his love is. I was passed out in my reclined seat and felt the car pull over. He quietly opened the door so I wouldn't wake up, and I felt him put a blanket over me. He was tucking me in. I had never felt so loved before. I thought, *Pinch me God, is this real? I never want to let this moment go.*

Ten months in, we were engaged and set a date to get married that winter. Everything happened so quickly, but I kept thinking, *It feels right.* As we were driving to see a wedding vendor one afternoon, a familiar song came on the radio: "Dream Come True." *No way,* I thought. *It's my song!* I closed my eyes to get lost in the moment. While I was daydreaming, he casually leaned over and whispered, "This would be an amazing wedding song, eh?" *Oh my gosh, yes,* I thought. *Yes!*

Our Big Day

"Today I will marry my best friend,
the one I laugh with, dream with, live for, love." -Author Unknown

Our wedding day was magical! A snowy winter wonderland, just as I always dreamed it to be. I felt like a snow queen with a long white cape, a fluffy muff, and tall white boots for pictures in the snow. It was perfect! The whole day was perfect. The moment that meant the most to us was saying our vows at the church. After the wedding was over, we were lying on a hammock in Jamaica, just soaking up our honeymoon and reflecting on the day. I mentioned those vows and said, "Wouldn't it be cool if every 25 years, or even every 10 years, we could go away to renew our vows?" Timmy responded immediately, "Ya, for sure! But that seems pretty long. Why don't we do it every five years instead?" *Oh my gosh,* I thought. *Okay!* We now have this beautiful tradition of renewing our vows as a family. No audience, no spectacle, just us and our kids. My dream is to one day be an old wrinkly lady like the one from *Titanic* and just look at this great big wall of photos, one for every five years. I love the thought of us growing old together and celebrating love as a family.

Our 5D Marriage

"Across the years, I will walk with you - in deep green forests; on shores of sand:
and when our time on earth is through, in heaven, too, you will have my hand." -Robert Sexton

One of the greatest joys of my life has been finding my best friend and marrying him. It has been 11 years and he's still the best guy I know. By no means are we perfect, but we *try* to be, for each other. The secret to our success is that we continue to keep each other first, especially in the thick of raising young children. What keeps it fun is that it still feels like we're dating. We complement each other, joke around all the time, schedule regular date nights, and hide cute love notes around the house, just like my parents did. We encourage each other to do a guy/girl night out to let go and have fun. When life gets hard, we lock arms and draw in closer. We pick each other up and choose to focus on the good. We've learned to admit fault, apologize quickly, and always forgive. If we do have a fight, it's kept private, as we never want the other to be looked down on. If we're simply feeling grumpy, we have a code word that means, "It's not you, I just need a moment." It saved us from so many potential arguments. Finally, we push each other to speak our truth, dream bigger, achieve our goals, and *grow as a person*. The happier we are as individuals, the happier we are as a married couple.

It's Waiting For You, Too

> *"Be the change you wish to see in the world."* -Mahatma Gandhi

Life didn't unfold as I thought it would, and yet, I wouldn't change a thing. The biggest lesson I've learned is that I could only attract love into my life once I was able to love myself first. I had to go deep within. Although it was scary to face my shadows and forgive them, doing so reclaimed my power and healed my soul.

My hope is that you're already in a happy and meaningful relationship. However, if you're unlucky like I once was, or just trying to add more love into your life, I hope this story inspires you to believe that anything is possible. You have the power to create love. Go within and determine what you want in your life. If that's love, embody love. If it's kindness, be kind. If it's happiness, work to make someone else happy. If you love the idea of sticky notes, be the first to leave one for your partner. Plant the seeds, water them, and watch how beautifully they grow. You have the power to change your circumstances, so become the change you wish to see in your relationship. Leave today knowing that happily ever afters *do* exist, and it's waiting for you, too.

About Stephanie Mahony:

Stephanie is a fighter, a spiritual warrior, and a cheerleader who inspires people to achieve their dreams.

She was born and raised outside of Toronto and graduated from university with a Bachelor of Commerce degree in Economics and Statistics. During her studies, she had an opportunity to do a student exchange program in Linz, Austria where she studied abroad and backpacked across Europe. Upon graduation, she decided to pursue her love of the stock market and began a career at one of Canada's top banks, where she's worked now for almost 20 years.

Stephanie is a wife and mother, now living her best life. She has a heart to serve her community and over the years has actively volunteered at her church, local hospital, animal shelter, as well as teaching financial literacy classes to new Canadian immigrants. For the last six years, she has also held the position of Vice Chair on the Board of Directors for a local non-profit organization. Most recently, Stephanie has opened up to new spiritual and healing modalities, such as reiki, and is completing a Lightworkers Certification program.

Stephanie is a speaker and best-selling author who is extremely passionate to help everyone around her live their best life. By sharing how she has overcome her own struggles, she hopes that it may inspire people to transform any obstacle in their way. Her goal is that they may dream bigger, live more confidently, and enjoy a life of abundance.

To connect with Stephanie:

Facebook: https://www.facebook.com/stephanie.mahony.50

Instagram: https://www.instagram.com/stephmahony/

Email: s.mahony82@gmail.com

The Awakening to Sovereignty

Marina Fabian

Faith and spirituality have always been guiding forces in my life. They aren't just a facet of my life; they are my whole life. Every bit of magic I have ever encountered are the effects of the Love and Light in which I act out of and connect with daily. When I was younger, I housed a ton of grief and anger from past family abuse as a child. I grew up being shamed and called names by my family, mostly about weight and worth. My heart felt like a spark of beautiful Light surrounded by a dark cave of uncertainty, fear, and trauma. Fortunately, I knew that I had a purpose and a path. Though the act of life felt like a ton of bricks on my shoulders, nothing was going to stop me from moving forward or working to heal and inspire the hearts of people and the world.

Through every bump in the road is an opportunity to grow higher and brighter. Whether that bump is an actual divot or a literal drop in the road that simply has to be leapt over to get to the other side, it's there to shine a light on a shadow. Trust me, I've had both at one point or another in my journey. Still, there couldn't be a clearer message than that in my life. Whether the challenge is miniscule or heart-wrenching, it is a seed of transformation waiting for us to tend to and explore. I was depleted beyond imagination. My heart felt like a wrung-out rag, my bones like rubble. Everything was an effort. If lost was the strongest word, I was incredibly lost.

One of the most difficult yet amazing experiences I have been through in my life is anorexia. So many voices and beliefs would swirl through my head daily. I believed them, yet wanted to prove them wrong. After years of health being an excruciating talking point and manipulation tactic, my wounded little heart found a way to control her environment and her body. Every morning and night, I would check in the mirror to make sure everything was perfect. Could I see my ribs? If I tilted my head back, could I see the ligaments in my neck? Were my hip bones pointing out? Great, then everything would be all right.

The months that passed by in this time swept away all of the Light and joy. My passion for life and self-care days when I would paint my nails were now replaced by starving hunger and fatigue. Empty. Everything felt so empty. I remember saying my prayers each day, desperately asking when I would feel like me, when I would feel powerful, and when people would care about me. In those moments, I thought all of the things I was doing would change the tides to bring all of that magic and change I was looking for. Unfortunately, that was not the case. One of the memories that will always be with me was that one day, I was so hungry that I actually ate bread scraps out of my compost bin. In my mind, it "didn't count." Clearly, my stomach being so empty was a mirror of how empty I felt inside. By universal law, however intense something is on the inside it will be mirrored on the outside. Looking back, eating out of my compost bin was a pretty strong example of that.

Feeling lost in my own heart and in my own sense of spirituality, I happened to be gifted a book. It was all about assertiveness, boundaries, and loving yourself from a spiritual standpoint for earth angels. This book opened the door for the Light to enter back into my heart. Literally right after reading it, I decided I had to quit where I was working. I was knee-deep in people pleasing, so it was a difficult conclusion to come to.

One of the most important beliefs that I am working to disintegrate is that I have to sell myself out for something, whether it's to gain someone else's approval, to not be left behind, or to have a need met. I can certainly say that belief was alive and well in my current work situation. My heart and soul really didn't want to be there after a while, and I would obsess about it all day. On the way to work, I would come down with heavy, full-body shakes. All of these things were revolving habits in my life, just placed in different scenarios.

Quitting wasn't easy at all. However, the day that I did, there was a sacred strength behind my choice. I was asked to change my mind about five times, but I didn't. I didn't sell myself out this time. I chose my heart, my soul, and what was best for *me*. It was an amazing taste of freedom and sovereignty. After leaving, I had more space to really float in what was going on in my body with the eating disorder. All I wanted to do was help myself and to be there for myself in ways I was told I hadn't been good enough in: my image and my health. There were so many prayers and tears in those months.

On a late September afternoon about five months after quitting my job, I was sitting on my leather sectional eating a plain sweet potato for dinner. I probably had green beans for breakfast and had snacked on as little granola as possible to get me through the day. I remember sitting there and instantly having a split-second breakthrough. I am no stranger to these breakthroughs. Usually, after enough sadness and abandon of who I am, my higher self has enough of it and there is an instant moment of clarity. I stepped back into my own spiritual and heart alignment. I realized I didn't want to hurt myself anymore because of other people's words. I deserved way more than that, even if I had to fight an internal battle to truly believe it. The sense of magic and innate truth had come back.

While I was in my recovery process, I found yoga. I did not expect to. Yoga had always been presented to me as relaxing and fluffy. My favorite workouts were the ones rooted in intensity and "seriousness." Naturally, anyone who is serious about being in shape needs to feel like they are dying after their workout; otherwise, you didn't try hard enough. Nine months after beginning the practice of yoga, I began the process to become a certified teacher. It was such an interesting experience and my first real foray back into working since shutting everything down and recalibrating my health. My motivation behind this choice was that I wanted the opportunity to teach, to heal, and to spread a message I believed in. It was everything my heart had ever wanted to do since I was born.

People were in my class to practice physically and to heal, along with my words and insight. I didn't want to feel abandoned if I was simply teaching knowledge and spiritual philosophies. I had this deep core belief that the spiritual insight and wisdom I felt so called to teach would be discarded, judged, and looked at as nonsense. Having yoga as the medium felt like such a safe and buffered way to share my words and wisdom. I taught yoga for a couple of years at a health club. During my time there I learned how to use my voice to a greater degree. I learned that there *are* people who wanted to see me. They felt inspiration and Love from my message. I learned what it was like to really step into your power, even in just the fledgling stages.

One of the things I am most proud of was once again listening to my heart, higher self, angels, and guides. One morning, I woke up and had another split-second breakthrough, which I now know and understand to be the soul and spirit calling me back into alignment. In that moment, I knew it was time to move on. I felt restricted in what I could share while teaching. I wanted to upgrade my message, to feel the freedom to share all of the magic and creation that is available to us as beings in an unfiltered way. So, I used my experience and skills I had built along the way, called on that learned, inherent courage, and lovingly parted ways with faith that I was right where I needed to be.

After that, I spent years of teaching and cultivating my voice. One of the biggest lessons in my life has been learning to feel safe in listening to myself. Even more than that, learning that it is *safe* to use my voice. Have you ever experienced that feeling of having a conversation with someone and wanting so badly for them to see you and hear you for your greatness and everything you have to offer? You want so strongly to share, but for some reason, the impact and magic just don't get shared or expressed completely. I don't know about you, but I usually feel a strong wave of defeat after that happens. It's hard. These are the times we have to go within, sit with the shadows, and ask the "why" questions. "Why does this feel like a block for me?" "Where have I experienced this before?" "When was the first time this showed up for me?" Plus, my favorite, "In what way can this help me to heal?" I've learned the interesting way that I simply do not have the choice to disregard my voice or higher self while still being in alignment.

For example, I was in a very uncomfortable spot last summer. My old wounds felt very unsafe. Rather than having faith that my higher self, which had a rather unconventional plan compared to other people's ideas, was correct, I chose to disregard it and act out of fear. In that choice, I started a new part-time job. Within the first 15 minutes, I repeat, *15 minutes* of that choice, I was bitten in the back of the leg by a giant dog. I cried, and you can bet I was bleeding. Even with literal blood and tears, I stayed in that situation for a whole week. These are the lessons and times that bring us back to Light, back to Love, and back to alignment. You'd think that would be enough of a reminder, right? Apparently, I was feeling very stubborn. I was still in this narrative of feeling like I had to sell myself out to have my needs met. Yet again, another instance of the non-negotiable call to *listen* to the voice and heart.

One day, I was feeling major resistance to go to a meeting. Looking back, I can honestly say I was skating by on autopilot and disassociating from how I actually felt. Well, I went to this meeting anyway, even though I felt like crying inside. Would you like to know what happened? Sure! I fell and broke my ankle, the ankle on the same side of my body as the gigantic dog bite from four months prior. I have only told a few people before now: even after knowing my ankle was badly hurt, I still abandoned my own voice and continued to physically work on the hurt foot, feeling I had to for someone else. However, I choose to forgive myself. The forgiveness is born from choosing to witness and understand our inner wounds to initiate the process of releasing the trauma and patterns. These examples are the physical reminders that we deserve to be happy, follow our hearts, and honor our wisdom and magic. Anything less than that is a compromise to the beauty of who we truly are.

In the end, I am grateful. I am grateful to myself first and foremost for always having my back and choosing to believe in faith, even when I forget and apparently need a physical reminder of what I am worth. I am grateful for all of the trauma and unbelievable cruelty that I have gone through. It was in these moments that I was shown exactly what I was not and the blindingly bright Light of who I am. I am grateful for the beautiful mentors and friends who have similar energy and backgrounds. I am so blessed to be connected to and have them as Soul Family. Without them, I am not sure I would have the same passion to bring healing and Light to everything I can. Who I am now is purely unrecognizable to who I was back then. I am still filtering out the aspects of my life that don't serve me and the beliefs that need rewiring. I now accept that it *is* safe to use my voice. My faith in myself is who I act for and serve for now, not the opinions or words of others.

I've learned that we aren't given experiences and circumstances in our own lives for no reason, they are given to us to learn and grow from. Each one of us has our own path. To step into the full authenticity of your expression and soul, you have to be willing to look deeply into all of the shadows and choose to bring them to the Light for yourself, your heart, your mission, and your purpose. Even in this moment while writing these words, I know that in six months, I will be an even stronger version of myself. That is the mission, and that is the calling: to wake up each and every day in the energy of Love, to hold ourselves in Grace, seek out the Truth, and be there for ourselves and others.

Today, I am working on developing my first online course. It will teach and inspire the aspects of creation while also expressing your True Self so that you may be in your highest alignment and bring healing to this world. To say I am proud of myself for that is an understatement. I am now a published author, a dream of mine forever. What I have found along my life's journey is the fact that *you* are the one. You are the one who knows you best, the one who gets to be your own best friend, and the one who has all of the power in the world to create the reality of your absolute dreams. You get to be the healer of and for you. What could be more magical than that?

About Marina Fabian:

Marina works with the principles of Sovereignty, Divine Quantum Healing, and the full utilization of the body and soul to create the container of transformation and fulfillment in life. As an Expressionist, it is her mission to inspire others to ignite their worth and power and embody it out into the world.

Marina is a channel here to awaken the innate radiance and wisdom in the creative healers and leaders of this world. She shines Light for the Light shiners. Using the wisdom from the fires of learned courage in order to bring in newer and higher frequencies and ways of living.

For those who know they have something huge to contribute to the collective, who feel the magic, love, and power flowing through their veins, she welcomes you into her circle.

Marina's over nine years of experience in energetic healing and accessing arts began with Angelic connections and healing. She is versed in several healing technologies including tarot, channeled writing, intuitive channeling and coaching, sound healing, and her personalized style of self-connection yoga.

Marina has always had an extremely strong connection to the heart space and uses that magical center as a springboard in all magical client work. She believes the most powerful source for transformation is everyone's own personal power and blueprint. She believes the chosen ones ready to up level in their mission and purpose deserve to be celebrated, expressed, and constantly transformed to their most aligned life and vision by the power of themselves.

Marina currently offers expression mentorship programs as well as upcoming group courses. If you feel a greater calling for your holy life, she invites you to connect!

To connect with Marina:
Instagram: https://www.instagram.com/marina.fabian/
Facebook: https://www.facebook.com/MarinaFabianPage
Website: https://www.marinafabian.com

Photo Credit: TruPhotography by Jaime
https://www.truphotography.me